I0110804

The Aborigine
AND THE
DROVER

JOHN P. F. LYNCH

Published in Australia by Sid Harta Publishers Pty Ltd,
ABN: 46 119 415 842
23 Stirling Crescent, Glen Waverley, Victoria 3150 Australia
Telephone: +61 3 9560 9920, Facsimile: +61 3 9545 1742
E-mail: author@sidharta.com.au

First published in Australia 2017
This edition published 2017
Copyright © John P. F. Lynch 2017
Cover design, typesetting: WorkingType (www.workingtype.com.au)
Cover Design by Luke Harris
Cover picture:
This is a sequel to the Novel — *The Convict and the Soldier*
The right of John P. F. Lynch to be identified as the Author of the Work has been asserted in
accordance with the Copyright, Designs and Patents Act 1988.

This book is a work of fiction. Any similarities to that of people living or dead are purely
coincidental.

All rights reserved. No part of this publication may be reproduced, stored in a retrieval system, or
transmitted, in any form or by any means without the prior written permission of the publisher, nor
be otherwise circulated in any form of binding or cover other than that in which it is published and
without a similar condition being imposed on the subsequent purchaser.

346pp

The National Library of Australia
Cataloguing-in-Publication Data
Lynch, John P. F.
The Aborigine and the Drover
ISBN 978-1-921030-97-0 (pbk)

To my Grandfather — Edmund Keough (born Keogh)
A Picneer of Kyneton and Tocumwal (Woodlea farm)
1866 — 1942

Contents

Foreword

This is a very interesting and entertaining novel which contains I am sure, many incidents of true escapades that occurred during the Victorian Colonial era. The author clearly has a love of early Australian history, and he has managed to weave a respectful and convincing relationship between settlers, ex-convicts and aborigines who in many cases, developed good working relationships with the European settlers.

The description of 19th century life at sea or in the outback, battling bushfires or shearing sheep — all go to show a genuine knowledge of how these activities were undertaken in those days.

We see through the eyes of the author the life of an ex-convict who made good, who rubbed shoulders with his peers and decent members of society from all walks of life and who achieved the rank of Commissioner of Crown Lands.

Life in Colonial Australia was tough whether you were a free settler, ex-convict or a former member of the militia — they were people who tamed the land and gave us the lifestyle and security that we all accept in Australia today.

This is a very readable book written by someone who clearly has an insight into the management, administration and politics of colonial Australia and who expresses it so well for all of us to learn and enjoy

Michael Garnett OAM ASM
Fellow Author

Introduction

The southern area of the Colony of New South Wales — the Port Phillip District — was destined to be the future city of Melbourne. It was settled in 1835 by John Batman and within weeks, he was followed by John Pascoe Fawkner and other pioneers from the town of Launceston in Van Diemen's Land (Renamed Tasmania in 1856). Within a few years, Melbourne had expanded rapidly, as did the exploration and settlement of the surrounding land. Many of the early pioneers were farmers from the British Isles. They found the land to be similar to areas in England and Ireland. Hence, they quickly claimed, settled and developed farms within fifty miles or more of Melbourne within the first ten years. The immigrants continued to rapidly expand throughout the colony from then on. In 1851, this large southern area was separated from the Colony of New South and named the Colony of Victoria.

The pioneers encountered many problems in pursuit of their dreams. These were mainly due to the confrontations and the problems of understanding the aboriginal race, the unknown terrain and its variable weather together with poor governance of the land allocation.

This story includes several true events and relates to the endeavours, tribulations and passions suffered by two men from different cultures, during this early period. One man was an Australian aborigine, the other an escaped Irish convict who had become a drover, a land owner and eventually, a person of note.

The Australian flora and the fauna, together with the

droughts, floods and bushfires, which are a part of Australia's life cycle, are vividly described together with the Victorian bush lands and animals.

This book is the sequel to 'The Convict and the Soldier.' I trust that readers will include this book in their personal library as a part of their Australian history collection.

John. P. F. Lynch
OAM KSJ JP FRVAHJ
'Highlands Village'
Craigieburn. VICTORIA.

Families

Mandu — the Elder
↓
Mondari ——————— TABU
and lubra Bunga
↓
Jimmy

Edmund Keogh and wife Hanna
(deceased)
↓
Maeve ——————— MICHAEL Keogh then Somerset—
Patrick & wife Mary Somerset (nee
Kirwan)
↓
Maeve-Ann——————Keogh (Somerset)

Joseph Hall and wife Anne
↓
JOHN————————David———————————Maryanne
and wife Maeve Hall (nee Keogh)
↓
John Jr —————————— Sean

CHAPTER ONE

The Aborigine

T he aborigine stood motionless, looking towards the distant horizon. The late afternoon sun was slipping below the horizon, creating brilliant rays of reds and yellows. It was doubtful if the aboriginal warrior cared one way or another about the magnificent view. He had seen the scene many times before. He always came to this rocky outcrop after his tribe had returned from a tribal fight. This time it was different. His first son, Mondari, had been killed and he had just buried him. The aborigine on the rocky outcrop was Mandu, a powerful Elder of the Yandarbee tribe.

The evening was quiet, even the birds and the rustling of the leaves were still. The only sounds were from the aboriginal camp lower down in the valley, made by the drone of the didgeridoo and the chanting of the lubras. Together they created a haunting and mystical air and created a calming effect on the tribe.

While tribal fights were common between the local tribes, it was unusual for a warrior to be seriously injured. Generally, the conflicts arose for trivial reasons, such as a tribal boundary that had been infringed during hunting. The reasons were soon forgotten after a short skirmish and generally there were only minor wounds from the spears or nulla nulla clubs. This time it was serious. Mondari had stolen a woman from the Banda, a distant tribe. The two tribes had little contact previously and the Banda wanted revenge. When Mondari heard that the other tribe had come looking for him and the woman, he told his father, who then assembled the warriors and marched out to meet them. This inter-tribal war would not be taken lightly. No tribe would accept the theft of their women without a battle.

Mandu's warriors soon found the Banda warriors, who had now intruded on their land. The two tribal war parties saw each other simultaneously and immediately started shouting and banging their spears on their shields. There was plenty of noise but little action initially. They gradually inched closer to each other then started throwing spears. The warriors easily avoided the spears from their opponents. They had been practising this art since they were young boys. The warriors now armed themselves with their nulla nulla clubs — small hard wood knotty section of tree branches and moved to engaged in hand to hand fighting.

Mondari and the other warriors of his tribe moved to intercept several of the opposition warriors, with arms swinging their clubs. Mostly they contacted the other warriors' wooden shields. The fight raged for about ten minutes until their arms started to ache and tire. Both sides stepped back for a minute or two, and then they charged at each other again swinging their clubs.

A group of intruding warriors had not joined in the initial fight and had been watching from a distance. When they saw that Mondari's warriors were tiring, they attacked. Mondari was the first casualty, he was attacked by three of this group of warriors and being out numbered, he had no chance of successfully defending himself.

He was struck on the head and immediately collapsed onto the ground. He was then struck several more times before the intruders quickly left the fight. Two other warriors from Mondari's tribe had rushed to his aid but were also injured, each suffering a broken arm.

When the Banda warriors realised that they had killed Mondari, they knew that the Yandarbee warriors would want revenge and would pursue them relentlessly, wanting to inflict the most violence on them. The Banda warriors had all ceased fighting and now fled, fearing for their lives. Their previous bravado was now a thing of the past.

Mandu and several of his warriors had been watching the fight on a hill overlooking the site. When Mandu saw what had happened, he immediately sent his warriors after the fleeing intruders. His warriors knew this country very well. They ran to intercept them by running across the fields to the top of a small gully, through which the intruders had to pass. As Mandu had anticipated, his warriors reached the high ground just as the Banda warriors entered the gully. The intruders were totally unprepared for the barrage of spears which stuck each of them. Six were killed immediately and the wounded intruders were also slain by being beaten with their nulla nullas. They were left where they fell. Vengeance had been both violent and complete.

Mandu hurried to the battle ground to find Tabu, his second son sitting by Mondari's body. Tabu was uninjured but he had been fighting near Mondari when he had been felled and had seen the fatal blows. The sound of his brother's skull being crushed, the subsequent gore and the further beating his brother had endured, had sickened him. Mandu looked at Mondari's injury, saying nothing to Tabu. He just picked up Mondari's body and walked towards the camp with the other warriors walking quietly behind him.

He carried his son back to an area close to their camp and immediately buried him, in the customary way. The warriors had dug a hole four feet deep. Mondari's body had been wrapped in his possum skins with his knees tied to his neck. He was then placed on his side in the grave. Several sheets of bark were placed over the body and the warriors then filled in the grave with soil. Finally, a pile of logs were lifted onto the grave to protect the body from wild animals. His spear was rammed into the ground at the head of the grave. His name would not be mentioned again.

The warriors were standing around the grave quietly and motionless. The only sound was the wailing of the Lubras, which was piercing and continuous. It was haunting and full of the hurt they were enduring for Mondari, their fallen warrior. Mandu appeared not to hear or see any of them.

Mandu's posture was one of standing very upright with his left foot on his right knee and his spear in his left hand. This stance, plus his small pointed beard and slooping forehead, gave him a most dignified air. His silhouette against the setting sun completed a perfect picture of a warrior. He continued to gaze at the far horizon and only moved when the sun had completely set below the far horizon. It was time to return to his camp. He did not want to go but he knew he had to return to his people, they would be lamenting as well. He must acknowledge his position as an Elder and sit with them

The track back to the aboriginal camp site was strewn with sharp shale rocks but he showed no discomfort as he walked. The soles of his bare feet were as hard as leather, after many years of walking on these types of rocks and stones. He sat silently at his small fire staring into the flames.

His tribe's camp site was in an open area, close to a river and consisted of several small fires and about twenty mia mia bark shelters. These shelters consisted of sheets of bark laid over several tree branches to form a tent-like structure. In extreme weather these were vacated with the tribe moving into their caves in the nearby ranges. Life was simple for them, the only time they knew was day or night and that of the dry and wet seasons when they moved these small camps as the season's climate or lack of food or water dictated.

Collectively, the tribe's only possessions were their hunting weapons, wooden cooking bowls, a few stone axes, possum skins and an occasional bark canoe. If they were lucky they may have obtained a sheep skin or two. If a white man approached, these were quickly hidden. The camp had a motley collection of dogs belonging to nobody in particular, but they helped keep the camp clean by eating all the scraps.

As a nomadic community, they had learnt how to live off the land as taught by their fathers who had learnt from their fathers before and so on. Normally, there would be a variety of food available from the forests. Grubs, wild bees, snakes and the larger animals such as wombats, kangaroos and lizards were also plentiful. Birds were on their menu. Root plants were found near the rivers and creeks. Frogs, fish and eels also from the river were easily netted by their reed baskets. At various times of the year grain or grass seeds were available and were ground in curved dish shaped rock with round rock.

While Mandu sorrowed, the lubras had cooked a large kangaroo in the coals of a large open fire. It was already being shared between the men, as he walked into the light from the fire. The other tribal members looked at him and fell silent. He knew it was he who should speak first. He raised his arm in a type of salute, went to the fire, tore off a rib of meat and went and sat down with his lubra following. She silently sat down next to him. The other members of the tribe continued with their meals, barely glancing in his direction.

Mondari was the firstborn son of Mandu, his mother had been captured during a raid on a coastal tribe. He had led a small raiding party in a canoe and had captured her when she was out fishing with other lubras. Her tribe could not chase Mandu as he had destroyed their canoes during the raid.

Mondari's brother, Tabu was born two years later. The

brothers had learnt to hunt in their early years. It was part of their childhood education. Their father made them small spears and together with a small pup they would play at hunting. The tribe's camp was at the foothills of a mountain range bordering a dense forest. The mountain and its surrounds hills were alive with native life, with no shortage of food or water. Mondari soon learnt to be a skilful hunter and grew to be a tall and fit warrior and was destined to be a leader of the tribe and now he was gone forever.

Tabu had been close to his brother and the shock of seeing his brother killed had caused him deep distress. Mandu had not spoken to him since. Tabu felt lost and with this loss came an urgency to go leave the tribe and go 'Walkabout'. Where? Anywhere!

Tabu left early morning without telling anyone, especially his father, who had continued to ignore him. Fully aware of the risks he could face, he headed south. The tribes north of his tribal grounds had a reputation of murdering strangers. He travelled lightly, carrying only a few possum skins, some spears, a nulla nulla and a small sharp flint stone for cutting up his captured animals or their cleaning skins.

The first few weeks he avoided everyone, and headed into the deep shrub country, only hunting when he was hungry and there were plenty of wildlife from which to choose. He enjoyed the serenity of the bush, together with the different bird calls. The shrill of the Lyrebird, the laughter of the Kookaburra and abundance of the smaller birds twitting on and on, had a calming effect on him as he tried to erase the memory of his brother's death from his mind. Eventually, he reached a rocky hill with a small cave underneath. It was at the crest of a valley. Here he decided to stay. For a month, he camped here, hunting, sleeping and watching the sunset, from dawn to dusk.

The sounds of horses and white men's voices echoed from down in the valley and curiosity made him venture out to see them. He had worked for white men before and spoke a few of their words. He cautiously clambered down the hillside, using the bush to hide his presence from the white men. When he reached the valley floor he saw an old track made by wagon wheel tracks and bullocks hoof marks. They had been made by timber cutters further up the valley. He followed the tracks from the hill side.

Just below him, two men were struggling to pull a wagon out of a muddy bog. They had dug trenches in front of the two front wheels and had cut logs to put in the trenches for the wheels to roll onto. He sat and watch from behind a tree. One man was in the wagon with reins, the other was trying to lead the horse. Each time he moved to lead the horse, the poles placed in the trenches were pushed out of the muddy trench. They needed a third person.

Tabu stepped out from behind the tree, without his spears and nulla nulla, the two men immediately grabbed their rifles from the wagon and levelled them at him.

Tabu said 'Hello Boss.'

The man holding the reins, said 'Who the hell are you, where did you come from?'

Tabu said 'I bin watchem yu bugger up.'

The other white man, after looking around the bush replied 'You help we give'm baccy.'

Tabu 'I speak good I helpum.'

They put their rifles back in the wagon. Tom, the man holding the reins thought the easiest job would be to lead the horse.

He pointed saying 'Pull reins when I yell out.'

His partner, Fred nodded. Tabu moved to the horse took hold of the reins and waited to be told; 'When!'

The two men placed the poles under the wheels and called 'Pull!'

Tabu pulled the reins but the horse didn't respond, he tried this several times. He then threw the reins over the horse's neck and jumped on its back and started shouting and whipping the reins. The horse suddenly came to life, started to pull and slowly the wagon moved forward until it was back on solid ground. The wheels had rolled onto the poles and up to the trench.

Tom was smiling and laughing and then asked 'Where did you learn to ride?'

Tabu replied 'Gulbin Riber Statin, I bin rousbout for sis muns.'

Tom and Fred leaned against the wagon and had a good look at Tabu. They saw a well built, young aborigine about six feet tall; clad with possum skins over his shoulders.

Tom said to Fred, 'He could help us by hunting for our food.'

Fred replied 'I was thinking the same.'

Tom asked Tabu 'You wantum work long us,' pointing to Fred and himself.

Tabu answered without speaking. He just nodded.

Fred went to the wagon and pulled out an old pair of trousers, saying to Tabu. 'Put these on, we don't want to see your prick hanging out all day.'

Tabu did as he was told and rolled his possum skins into ball and threw them onto the wagon. He had worn trousers before at Gulbin Riber. That boss has said the same. Fred pointed to the wagon. Tabu climbed up and made a seat for himself, between the shovels, dishes, buckets, wooden planks and more.

Tom Williams and Fred Wyland had been friends for over ten years and had decided to seek their fortune together — they knew not how? But seek they would — maybe gold mining? The wagon continued up the timber cutters track, bouncing and rolling continuously with the three of them hanging on tightly. The journey finished as the sun was setting over the hills and they had stopped in a small clearing. They could see where timber had previously been felled. The forest had been cleared for around twenty acres. They had been big trees and there were still many more. But the timber cutters had moved on.

Tom and Fred decided to continue driving for one more day. They found the going much harder after the timber cutters track finished. Fred decided to set up camp in the lee of a large granite wall. They were both excited when they started picking up rocks and breaking them into smaller pieces.

They began to build a small two room shack of bark and saplings, filling the gaps with mud. The horse had a large grass area to himself. After being tied to a long line and being provided with a water bucket he just grazed and slept.

It was a very tranquil area with abundant bird life and other wildlife, Possums, Wallabies and Wombats etc. Within two weeks the shack was finished, with some rough furniture made, a water stream located and Tabu had stocked the larder using his hunting skills. He slept under a tree, where he preferred to be. He had killed, cleaned and skinned the animals as the white men did. Tom then salted the meat to stop it from becoming rancid.

Tabu wondered why the white men had come here? They spoke very little to Tabu. This did not concern him, he was by nature a reserved person, but he listened to their words and began to learn more of their language. He had known some words and now would soon be able to put a sentence together.

He began to understand why they had come here, when Fred and Tom had unloaded the wagon and laid out the goods on the ground, Tabu started to remember. He had seen Gold diggers before on his father's tribal lands but they left after two months. Tabu knew that a pick and shovel were used to dig holes but not the use of the smaller picks and dishes. He was unfamiliar with some of the other goods that they had brought with them.

Time dragged on, Fred and Tom wandered around the immediate camp site day after day, looking at rocks, until one day when Tabu was out hunting, he suddenly heard the sounds of digging. He arrived back in the camp and found Fred and Tom working, one swinging a pick and the other shovelling soil and digging a hole. He sat and watched them, every now and then they would pick up a piece of rock and use the small pick to break up the rock into smaller pieces

After both of them had closely examined the rock pieces they would shake their heads, throw away them and start digging and winching up more rocks. This routine continued for a month and nothing changed.

The hole was now over twenty feet deep and the soil and rocks being dug out had changed from a deep brown colour to a light brown. This had excited them and they continued to work longer hours into the night.

Tabu heard their shouts as he sat beneath his tree. Tom was first to the surface with Fred close behind.

He heard them shouting. 'It's gold! It's gold!'

They danced around yelling and shouting. They sat down at the table, looking at the large rock they carried up from the hole. It was both white and light brown with a line of gold running through the entire rock. It was an inch wide in one part.

Tabu was unable to share their excitement as his way of life had no monetary value.

Fred looked at Tabu and said 'You have no idea what this means to us, have you, if you only knew?' Tabu had a good idea.

After extracting the gold from the rock quartz over the next month, they had dug out and winched up enough gold to half fill their water canteen. This was a small fortune for them both. They decided to dig for one more week and then leave to find a gold assayer to value their gold and then to enjoy life. The pit was now over thirty feet deep and the pit sides were crumbling a little. It concerned Fred, but Tom wanted to continue until the end of the week as agreed.

Fred climbed to the surface, he had enough digging. He came over and sat next to Tabu saying. 'You can have whatever you want from our stocks. Do you understand me? You take'm.'

Tabu understood, but he had little or no use for any of the stock. He just nodded to Fred. He had been thinking to leave them soon and to go walkabout again. He had been in this valley with them for over two months. He had listened and had learnt their language and was now reasonably fluent but with a deep slurred accent. He watched and saw how they related to each, their manners, the way they dressed, how they showed their emotions.

His race was stoic, showing very little of their feelings. During his previous walkabouts, he had worked with the white men, but had learnt very little of their culture, as he had not been interested. Yes! He had learnt to ride a horse, shear sheep and a few words of English. This time it was different, he had changed since his brother's death. He sensed a new direction for his life.

A muffled sound made both Fred and Tabu turn and look. A cloud of dust rose into the air. Fred shouted 'The mine!' and they both started to run towards the dust cloud.

When they arrived, they could see that one side had collapsed. Tom was nowhere to be seen. The ladder was still intact, Fred panicked and started to climb down the ladder. He did not look or he would have realised that one side of the winch was unsupported and was about to topple into the pit. Suddenly the winch tilted and tipped, and fell down into the pit. Fred saw it coming and tried to climb back. But he had no chance, the winch hit his left lower leg.

Tabu saw what had happened and climbed down the ladder

and lifted Fred to the surface. As soon as he got Fred out of the pit, he could see that the lower leg was badly damaged. It was bent and obviously broken. Tabu looked down the pit and could see that the pit was half full of soil. Tom was buried alive, he was beyond help.

Tabu helped Fred to the shack. After cutting away his trousers he could see that both lower left leg bones had been broken. Fred was in a lot of pain but was able to tell Tabu what he must do. He had served in the Colonial Forces in the Maori Wars and knew basic medical treatment. He had seen broken legs set several times. He knew that the leg must be put into a splint.

He sent Tabu to cut two sections of strong bark about the length of a man's arm and to find some rope in the wagon. Tabu soon returned with the bark and the rope. Fred showed him what to do. He then told him that the leg must be straightened before the bark is placed around the leg. He asked Tabu to give him a leather strap and told him, no matter what happens he must pull the leg straight before he put on the splint. Fred bit on the strap and nodded to Tabu to pull the leg. Tabu did not want to pull on the leg and just stood there.

Fred took the strap from his month and roared at Tabu. 'Do it!'

Tabu took a deep breath and pulled and pulled again until the leg looked straight. Fred had first bitten the strap hard and gone pale and then he passed out. When he came round, the splint was in place. He was still in great pain. There was Laudanum in the wagon. He asked Tabu to get the bottle and pour him a dose of the pain relief mixture. It helped a little but then shock had set in and Fred had to fight for himself.

He had Tabu wrap him in blankets and saddle cloths. Fred was fit, so he knew he had a good chance of recovery. Tabu sat by his side for two days until he had recovered from the effects of shock.

What to do now? Fred knew that there was no sense in

delaying their departure. Nothing could be done for Tom and his leg needed to be looked at by a doctor as soon as possible. He asked Tabu to load the wagon and harness the horse. The horse had grown fat and lazy in the grassy paddock but it would be fit.

After Tabu gave Fred a drink of water and a meal of meat and potatoes, they started travelling at daylight, retracing their path of two months ago. There had been no rain since then but the ruts and holes were still there, Fred suffered further pain from the jolting of the cart but it could not be avoided.

After three days, they reached the open plains and the going became much easier, they eventually reached a road. The sign post said — Kilmore 3 Miles.

They continued into Kilmore, stopping when Fred saw the writing on a hoarding 'Gold Assayer'. Fred asked a bystander to get the Assayer to come to see him. He came out and Fred spoke with him. An animated discussion ensured, he then handed over his gold and after it was weighed and assayed, Fred duly received a handsome cheque. Tabu then drove Fred to the Bank of New South Wales where the cheque was immediately deposited. The bank manager treated Mr. Frederick Wyland as a life-long friend. He needed Fred's custom, the banks were fiercely competitive.

The sign said — Hospital and Medical Doctor. Again, Fred asked a bystander to ask the Doctor to come out.

The Doctor exited his office door with an angry look on his face and said 'You come to me, I don't go to you!' 'What do you want?'

Fred said 'I want you to fix my broken leg.'

'What another penniless miner, go away.' ordered the Doctor.

Fred replied 'I have money and I can pay now.'

'Well that's different. Bring him in' said the Doctor to Tabu.

Tabu helped Fred into the Doctor's surgery and sat him on the table.

The Doctor said 'Thank you, you can go now.'

Tabu nodded to Fred and left the Doctor's premises. Tabu went to the wagon and picked up his possum skins and weapons and walked out of the town of Kilmore up into the hills, alone again.

After the Doctor had given Fred's leg a detailed examination, he remarked 'Your leg will be fine again in a few months, you will have a slight limp, whoever pulled the leg straight and put on the splint did a good job. Who did it?'

'The aborigine who brought me in' replied Fred. 'I must see him.'

'What! I don't believe it and anyhow he's gone now,' said the Doctor.

'It's true, believe me. Are you sure that he has gone?' queried Fred.

Fred could not believe that he had missed saying thanks and goodbye to Tabu. Fred had not realised that walkabouts are spontaneous. He would miss Tabu, just having him around was good. He had asked for nothing and had taken nothing offered.

It was saddening for Fred, as he knew he would now need to adjust his life after losing both Tom and Tabu together so soon. He still had the Gold mine which only he and Tabu knew its whereabouts and he trusted Tabu. How could he not — he had saved his life, he would have died without his help. Maybe one day he would have the chance to repay the debt.

Tabu had changed his trousers for his possum skins. He kept the trousers — they may be needed again one day. He headed west along the mountain range. It was densely forested with no shortage of wildlife. There was another tribe in this area with who he had no contact, so he needed to be careful. He was enjoying his freedom from commitments, no hunting or cooking for others.

He would sit by the creeks watching the trout and the agile platypus at play. The platypus was so different from other animals with their duck-like bill, webbed feet and flat rounded tail. They lived in underwater holes and suckled their young. He hadn't caught one but as a young boy he had been told of the poisonous claw inside their rear legs. Besides, there were plenty of less dangerous animals to catch for food. Tabu spent a few days up in the mountains then decided to on. Where? He just started to walk.

Tabu began to move through the dense mountain range to the west. He would walk a few hours each day then camp in a cave or clear a small area in dense brush. He could see out but he was invisible to man and animal alike. Sometimes he would stay for a week or so, content with his own company. After a few months, he had gradually moved down to a valley, which opened onto flat open plains where he knew there were farms. Why, he did not know, perhaps he should be with people again and maybe work for them?

The valley was filled with mist for as far as he could see. Only the tops of the tree lined hills were visible. The sun was shining and the trees glistened with their early morning dew. A few birds were noisily completing the picture. The mist had gone within the hour and revealed several farm houses in the distance, with grazing livestock and sown grain fields.

Eventually Tabu reached a bush track and he could see a farm house nearby. He continued to walk down the track wondering if he should ask the farmer for a job.

CHAPTER TWO

The Drover

Tabu was walking down the country track, with his head down when he heard a white woman's voice. He looked up and saw a horse and rider. They were travelling fast towards him. Suddenly he realised that the horse had bolted and that the rider was a woman. She was holding onto the saddle pommel for 'dear life'. They were coming down a narrow stretch of the track with bushes on either side. Tabu was hidden from their view. He decided to interrupt the path of the horse when he judged the distance was close enough to jump into its path and hopefully shock the horse into slowing down so that he could grab one of the loose reins.

He waited until he judged what he considered to be the correct distance and jumped into its path. The horse saw Tabu and reared up, he grabbed a rein and pulled the horse's head down. The rider had slipped down the horse's rump, when it reared and had rolled away. Tabu soon had control of the horse and tied it to a tree.

He then went to the lady who was sitting on the ground and looking around her with a dazed expression on her face.

Tabu asked 'Oriht Missus?'

Mary Somerset didn't answer at first. She looked at him rather vaguely and then she asked 'Could you help me up please?'

Tabu did as he was asked and waited to see what she wanted to do. He could see a homestead on the hill, within easy walking distance.

He said 'I takem horse em you long house' as he pointed to the homestead.

The woman nodded and mounted her horse. Tabu untied the reins and led the horse back down the lane.

Michael Somerset was sitting on the veranda and in the distance saw the horse walking, and suddenly realised that something was wrong. Why would Mary be in the saddle with an aborigine leading the horse? Michael hurried down to meet them.

As soon as Mary saw Michael she swooned and nearly fell from the saddle.

Michael caught her and helped her to the veranda.

Mary said in a whisper 'It was him' pointing to Tabu. By this time Dinny, his general hand, had arrived and took the horse's reins.

Michael turned to Dinny and yelled 'Grab him and lock him in the stable.'

Tabu started to say something but stopped and said nothing, he was too surprised!

Michael carried Mary to their bedroom and laid her down. He sat beside her. She had started to come to her senses and reached to hold Michael saying 'I was so frightened. He wouldn't stop.'

Michael asked 'Did he hurt you?'

'No, but my back is very tender from my fall,' she replied

'You can tell me all about it when you rest up and feel better. I have him locked up in the stable.' He said. Mary relaxed then closed her eyes and went to sleep

Michael went to the stable with Dinny and angrily fronted up to Tabu asking 'What did you do to my wife?'

Michael was surprised when the aborigine answered in good English saying 'I help bring'm missus to house, she fall from her horse, she good?'

Michael looked at him and said 'You stay here until my wife wakes up and tells me what happened.' He and Dinny then turned and walked out of the stable. Dinny locked the door behind them.

Michael sat in his study waiting for Mary to awake. She came into the room two hours later again calm and collected and went over to Michael and kissed him.

Michael started speaking 'Well you have had an eventful day and appeared to have handled it very well. What happened?'

'If it hadn't been for the aborigine, it could have been much worse. Where is now?' she asked.

'He's locked up in a stable,' he answered.

'Why? He possibly saved my life. He stopped my bolting horse and brought me home. I want to see him!' Mary insisted.

'We'll both go and see him,' said a surprised Michael.

They quickly walked to the stable, unlocked the door. Mary went in first 'I'm so sorry, are you alright?' She asked.

Tabu stood up in his possum skin and said slowly 'I 'oriht' Mary blushed and looked away.

Michael was puzzled by this man. He was no ordinary aborigine. He stood tall and proud and had learnt English yet he wore possum skins.

He said 'Thank you for helping my wife.' Michael then asked him 'Are you hungry?'

'Yes, Tabu hungry,' replied Tabu

'I'll send you some food, you can stay here if you wish. I'll be back in a few days after I have finished some shearing and we will talk.'

Michael and Mary left Tabu to his thoughts. They both felt uncomfortable over the misunderstanding. Tabu had taken off his possum skins and put on his only pair of trousers. Dinny had entered the stable to collect harnesses and greeted Tabu who had nodded in response. It was a good start, if Michael was to offer him a job, this man would probably be his boss.

Michael pushed the last of the shorn sheep down the chute into the holding pen, where the roustabout caught the sheep, branded them and looked for any cuts from the shears. These he would dab with tar to protect the sheep from the notorious blowflies, which would infest the wounds and could cause the animal to eventually die. This would be his last contract for this year, the shearing season was now finished.

The fleeces had been sorted and pressed into their bales, they would now be loaded onto large wagons and hauled to the port at Hobson Bay, destined to sail to the English port of Liverpool and hence to the knitting mills in Manchester. Michael believed that the wool from the Kyneton district should be sold direct to the Mills with fewer middle men involved. He needed to explore some options. Perhaps he should go to Manchester in person and see what could be done?

Michael Somerset and his three-part time shearers had shorn a thousand sheep. His two young roustabouts were hard workers. Their other jobs were to pick up the fleeces from the shed floor. They then rolled the fleece and lifting it up in their arms, they flung the fleece up, flicking it open to making it fall flat onto the sorting table for grading. They also sweep the floor and collected the smaller off cuts of the belly wool and the crutchings. The shearing sheds had the not unpleasant smell of lanoline from the wool. The workers' clothes soon became greasy and their hands were always smooth, from handling the wool, due to the lanoline.

This shearing contract had gone smoothly with the rain holding off. Wet weather helped no one, the owners, the shearers or the fleece pressers. Wet fleeces were difficult to shear; they would smell and reduce the quality and could make for extremely heavy wool bales that could mislead buyers. Fortunately, they had enjoyed mild temperatures and the job had been completed in just four working days. Michael as the contractor was responsible to leave the shearing shed tidy. He had made a final check of the shed to see if they were leaving it neat and all with the equipment back in its place, satisfied, he closed the door and headed up to the homestead.

The owner of the property, William Eden and he had been friends since Michael arrived in Kyneton seven years ago. William stood on the veranda as they walked up to the homestead, he invited them all to join him. He had anticipated that they would finish today and had his wife arrange a table of food and drink to mark the end of the shearing. William and his wife had been in the area for nearly ten years. They had made a success of their farm, starting it from nothing. They bought eighty acres of mainly scrub and then took two years to clear it and plant their first crop. It had been successful and they then bought a further four hundred and eighty acres. Sheep and a few cattle now completed their rural scene.

Several years ago, William and his wife had experienced the ultimate horror of the death of their son due to an armed robbery. The coach, they were travelling in, was 'Bailed up' by bushrangers on a bridge crossing the Campaspe River at Kyneton, when the river was in flood. Two bushrangers stopped the coach on the bridge. One bushranger ordered the passengers out while the other watched the driver, pointing his shotgun at him. After leaving the coach, the six passengers including William, his wife and son Eric were lined up.

The bushranger watching the driver moved towards the passengers, taking his eyes off the driver, when suddenly the driver whipped up the horses to move out. Eric, who was nearest the open coach door, ran to get in. The other bushranger kicked the door closed and the metal edge of the door severed two of Eric's fingers.

The boy screamed and ran to the other side of the coach as the horses reared. The coach hit the boy, who then fell between the bridge rails into the flooded river. The bushrangers saw what had happened and immediately rode away.

William ran to the side of the bridge looking over — Eric had vanished in the swollen and raging river waters. Nothing could be done. His body was never found.

His wife grieved for a long time. The Eden's later had two other children and eventually they had got on with their lives. Eric was not forgotten — his picture has pride of place in their hall entry.

Michael had become a respected farmer and drover who had had success with breeding Merino sheep and had become in demand as a contract shearer He had hired a permanent general hand for his farm and had his three-part time shearers and young roustabouts to assist him with his contract jobs. They were reliable and good workers. He would use them again. He had an active and content life.

Michael loved the open air and carefree life. Often at times when working in the paddocks he would sadly remember his late friend Seamus Lynch who had been killed by aborigines near Kilmore.

Seamus and he had become itinerant shearers after escaping from the Van Diemen's Land Port Arthur Penal establishment. A local farmer, Albert Somerset and his wife, whom they had helped in their hour of need, had reciprocated and given them a job and Albert had taught them how to shear.

He and Seamus had then escaped to Victoria and eventually they purchased their Kyneton farm 'Woodlea.' When Seamus had died, Michael invited his sister Mary, to come to Kyneton. Michael and Mary married a year after his funeral, at a simple service at St Mary's Catholic Church in Kyneton. Michael had used his adopted name of Somerset on the marriage certificate. Mary knew of his past. He wished it could have been his birth name — Keogh, but it would have been too risky.

After paying off his shearing team, Michael headed for home. It had been a good contract. They had become financially secure with his shearing and droving tasks and the farm provided most of their food needs. Life was good for the two of them.

On his return, Mary handed him a letter, received from a large station holder named Hedley Rooke on the Murray River in the Colony of New South Wales. He wished to purchase two of Michael's best rams and a small flock of his Merino ewes and could he arrange delivery? Mr. Rooke needed to start a second flock and he wanted new rams for his current flock.

He had heard of Michael's success at the Kyneton Agriculture Show where Michael had won four prizes due to the quality of his rams. One ram was Grand Champion in the fine wool class. Michael sat thinking about the possible sale. His rams were due to be changed, he had had them for over two seasons and he also had ewes available for sale. He wouldn't need long to consider the request.

He hadn't travelled to the Murray River yet but he had reports of good lands on the river flats. He decided to sleep on the idea to ensure he was fully comfortable with the idea of travelling to the distant and newly explored district.

Michael had heard a few stories praising the lands north of Heathcote all the way to the Murray River, but they were always second or third hand. As a farmer, he was interested in acquiring quality land property. If the stories were true, then the lands north could be worth exploring. It would be the only way he would know for sure. If he decided to go to Echuca, perhaps that would be the time to explore the area and see for himself.

The following morning, he did a tour of his property with Dinny who brought Tabu with him, who looked and listened. The fences were in good condition, the ones damaged by the seasonal high winds and heavy rains had been repaired. The dams were all nearly full. The fallen trees cut and stacked and the ruts in the roads had been filled with small rocks and then packed with clay/mud. Dinny was a good worker.

Michael turned to Tabu and asked? 'What jobs doum long u?'

Tabu answered 'I chop, I ride, I wok hard.'

Michael turned to Dinny saying 'Take Tabu to Kyneton on horseback today and bring back the gig with the repaired wheel. See how he handles the horse at a canter and at a gallop.' He waved to them and then walked back into the farmhouse for lunch with Mary.

He discussed the question with Mary concerning his possible venture to the New South Wales Border to deliver and sell the sheep. Mary would have preferred him to stay home but Michael was still a young man looking for challenges, such as was this district to new settlers. She suggested that he go, who knows he may find his good grazing land?

Dinny returned driving the gig and with Tabu riding along-side him. Michael looked at Dinny, who nodded, 'He can ride. He's good.'

Michael smiled and said 'Good, that's what I wanted to hear. Tabu, do you want a job?' Tabu just nodded.

Michael had decided to deliver the rams and ewes to New South Wales. He started planning that very afternoon. He would take the shearing wagon to carry the rams, the food supplies and camping equipment. He employed another drover Stan, who was single and unemployed. He and Tabu would accompany Michael, together with the two rams they would take four horses, two dogs and twenty ewes.

He estimated it would take them around a fortnight to the border with the wagon. They should average ten miles a day. The owner would meet them at the Port of Echuca which was on the south bank of the Murray River border crossing and he would be paid on delivery.

Michael would decide if he wanted cash or a bank draft depending on what he saw on the journey northward and anything of value worth buying to bring home — a land agreement or sheep or maybe nothing! He was interested in inspecting other Merino sheep if he could find a good flock or two. Perhaps he could purchase a fresh ram or two and maybe some ewes.

As usual, he had a tearful farewell with Mary. He told her to promise to go and visit Maeve and his father each fortnight and to keep the other dogs inside with her at all times. Dinny slept in a room at the big barn only fifty yards from the main house and he was trustworthy. Mary would be safe.

The journey started slowly winding down the river road over the bridge and up the other side and then heading due north. The roads albeit tracks were easy to follow, the wheel tracks could be seen for miles winding through the tall grasses and ground cover. The earlier pioneers' heavy wagons wheels had crushed the tussocks and any other ground growth. Michael's party left the road frequently to avoid the deepest ruts, some were still full of water and this was summer.

The countryside was flat mostly with clumps of shrubs that were often emptied of their bird life, with a splendour of colour and sound, when disturbed by the sounds of the wagon and sheep.

At times Michael would lie across the seat of the wagon and watch the wedge tail eagles floating on the wind, soaring and diving in the clear blue sky. Other times the quietness of the bush would be filled with the sound of the Laughing Jackass — The Kookaburra. What a magnificent sound. Sometimes, as if in revolt, the sulphur crested Cockatoos would shriek raucously and create an absolute din, abusing one's hearing. A stark contrast to the Kookaburras delightful sounds.

They camped the first night, under a clear starry night sky with a light northerly wind, at peace with the world. When they awoke the next morning, the wind had freshened and Michael could see smoke to the north-west. Tabu pointed and said 'You lookum boss.' Michael nodded and started to pack the wagon. They fed the sheep, the horses and the dogs and then after a hearty breakfast, they harnessed their horses without delay and moved northwards.

After three hours, they stopped and rested and tendered the animals. They could see a small inn and several houses up further, probably an hour or so to travel and decided to head there. The smoke had intensified and the wind had not abated. Michael knew the inn was on a small river, so it was the haven they needed to decide if they would be at risk with a bush fire.

As they approached the inn, they could see several other wagons nearby, with people standing around anxiously looking towards the smoke. Michael and Stan knew several of the farmers and they each nodded without comment.

They all had one thing on their mind — how dangerous would the fire be? It was the end of summer; the district had experienced high temperatures and low rain fall. On top of that situation, there was the hot strong northerly wind. A recipe for disaster and the fire appeared to be heading towards them.

He could see men ploughing in the large paddock all the way down to the river bank then turning around and repeating the ploughing in the opposite direction. The paddock was between the inn and the fire.

Old Bill the Innkeeper walked over and shook hands with Michael and Stan.

'Hello Michael, we've been watching this fire for three days. It's been tracking along the river and hasn't crossed it due to the wind direction. I have had some local boys ploughing a fire break on my field for half a mile across since then. They will probably have two hundred yards cleared for half a mile if or when the fire arrives. We plan to keep at it until the fire arrives.'

Old Bill paused and wiped his brow. 'We're ploughing from the river bank to the west and hope to have the fire break with virtually nothing in the paddock to burn. The buildings should be safe in the area between the river and the fire break. I'll call out if we need some help from you.'

Michael nodded — What more could he say? Old Bill walked away.

The horses could smell the smoke and had become very excitable. Michael headed with them towards one of the big barns. They unharnessed the horses and together with Tabu, led them into the darkness where he saw several other stabled horses and a farm hand. Stan stayed with the sheep.

The farmhand said 'I know what you are thinking. I've already tied up my horses and blindfolded them. They'll go berserk if you don't blindfold yours. I saw it happen in another fire. We had to shoot one horse.' The farmhand shook his head saying. 'It wasn't a pretty sight.'

Michael asked. 'Who do I see for permission to use the barn?'

'Me. My dad owns the barn. You can leave them here. I'm Jamie.' Michael shook hands and thanked Jamie.

After they secured the horses, he brought in the two rams and tied them up with a make shift harness around their necks, behind the front legs and up over the backs. He would not allow the rams and the ewes to be kept together.

The three of them and the dogs left to join the other men. Several other horses were already stabled. As with most small settlements, there were several sheep holding yards near the buildings. These were situated between the few houses and the inn. Stan soon drove the ewes into a yard with help from the two dogs.

Old Bill seemed to be the leader and was holding a crisis meeting. Michael later learnt that he had been a soldier in the Crimean War.

He queried 'What can we do if the fire starts jumping the fire break?'

One of the local timber cutters said. 'Fight the ground fires that may start outside of the ploughed area.' He had several poles at his feet with pieces of an old sail attached to one end.

Old Bill said 'What do we do with them?'

The head timber cutter answered. 'You plunge them into a barrel of water and then hit the fire or embers with the canvas section.'

Old Bill responded 'What if we have no water?'

'You still belt the fire, this helps to break up ground fires, I've seen them used before and they definitely work,' the timber cutter said.

Old Bill asked 'Any other ideas?'

'Yes. Collect any loose rubbish, branches, shrubs and whatever that is around the inn and the houses that will burn and chuck'm into the river. We only have to carry it a few yards,' said a voice from the rear.

There were ten men altogether and three women with four children all under ten years of age. Old Bill called the ploughmen to return from the paddock. The men then removed the plough and attached a sled in its place. On this they placed four barrels filled with water and towed them to the ploughed section near the river and then they distributed them at intervals of about fifty yards, along the edge of the ploughed paddock nearest the buildings. They were only able to repeat this twice as they only had twelve barrels. The barrels were covering half the ploughed area from the river edge. The river end was the more critical section.

If the fire crossed at the river junction, the buildings and perhaps they themselves would also be in trouble. Surprisingly, not one person had considered leaving the settlement.

The clean-up was a revelation, after two or so hours of labour, the settlement was spic and span. Old Bill doubted if anyone realised how much unnecessary rubbish had been allowed to accumulate around the inn, the houses and barns, over the past years. It was the subject of much good-natured banter between the men and the women and helped ease the tension from the ever-threatening bush fire.

The waiting was difficult. They drank tea, talked of their families, strolled around looking towards the fire and checking the wind direction and stared idly into space. They expected the fire to arrive tomorrow. Try to sleep! Impossible! The skyline was a beautiful and yet a forbidding mixture of red and various shades of yellow. It was awesome to see, but did not encourage one to sleep.

Dawn had arrived complimented by the local rooster announcing its arrival. Most of the people were already up and about, many with a cup of tea in one hand and a cigarette in the other; strange — with a bushfire around.

The women were busy preparing breakfast. The smoke was now stronger and appeared closer. The one blessing was that the wind had abated and it was now only a light breeze. But it was still of concern!

Old Bill had arranged the men into teams. Michael, Stan and Tabu were to be positioned at the river corner of the paddock, down near a barn. They had their poles with canvas attached and stood near a water barrel, while the other teams were at intervals standing along their water barrels. An extra man was a lookout on the roof of the highest barn and called down the advance of the fire.

The lookout advised loudly. 'The fire's tracking along the river bank on our side and the fire break. It appears to be heading away from the settlement.'

Trees along the river bank could be seen erupting into flames accompanied by loud explosions, but no major fires had started near the fire break area, other than very small fires which lasted only a few minutes then smouldered into small puffs of smoke

The main fire had been controlled by the fire break, but more trees along the river bank could be seen catching fire and could possible create a major problem.

Old Bill yelled to the timber cutters to grab their axes and chop down as many trees as possible and getting them to fall into the river. They ran forward from their posts and starting hacking and loping any greenery on the bank. Michael and watched them in action. Their muscles rippling with sweat dripping as they swung their axes with fury. They balanced their bodies with their feet feeling for a firm grip on the bank or a branch. They were twenty feet apart from each other, immediately they cleared one area they moved forward to another area, towards the fire.

Michael heard Old Bill call his name. He immediately turned towards him. Old Bill pointed to the top barrel. Tabu was at the barrel wetting the canvas.

Embers had been blown in by the wind and had started a small grass fire near the barn. Tabu and Stan were soon thrashing the grass sending small fiery weeds into the air. These soon extinguished themselves but they had to be dispersed first by being hit hard and often with the canvas poles. Michael turned to the barrel and plunged the canvas into the water and then ran to assist. With the three of them thrashing the small fires, they were soon in control of the situation. Several small fires continued to occur outside the fire break but were all extinguished by dispersing them using the wetted canvas poles.

The heat from the river bank fire soon got too hot for the timber cutters and they had to withdraw. However, they had succeeded in cutting the bank free of trees and brush for about fifty yards. With Michael and four others handling any small fires nearing the settlement, Old Bill and the remaining men would fight the fires on the river bank. The timber cutters had effectively cut a fire break, the exploding trees often sent showers of sparks and live embers sky wards. These men were also able to disperse the embers by thrashing them with their trusty wet canvas poles.

The smoke was slowly billowing through the settlement and carrying ash which no one could avoid. The fire fighters' eyes were smarting and stinging, swabbing them with cold water helped for a short time but generally they accepted the irritation.

It was more important to save one's possessions, no matter what value they were. They were yours. Each of them fighting the fire believed that they would survive the fire. Such was their attitude or was it their belief in their own Almighty, even Tabu.

By late afternoon the main fire front had passed to the south and although the small work force heaved a collective sigh of relief, they were kept busy extinguishing every ember, smoldering twig, smoking tussock or anything suspected of being hot and easily ignitable. Old Bill was everywhere looking and shouting orders. Eventually he called a halt and invited the ladies to prepare some tea and sandwiches.

Most of the men preferred something stronger and Bill tabled a dozen cold bottles of beer and two bottles of homemade lemonade. The workers sat on the ground alongside the big barn, even though the ground was still very warm. They said very little to each other at first. It took a beer to start the conversation.

Old Bill said to the head timber cutter. 'Your canvas poles worked well, they did the job.'

He answered 'Yes, they were good but the fire break was what saved the day. We may not have won without it. But we should have cut down those overhanging trees, at the end of the ploughed strip, much earlier.'

Old Bill nodded saying 'Well all's well that ends well.'

The timber cutter stood up and said. 'Don't forget to keep a watch overnight to ensure no spot fires start. I've seen buildings catch fire twelve hours after all the fires were supposedly out.'

Late afternoon the settlement was nearly back to normal. Michael, Stan and Tabu had a meal of bread and meat with a pannikin of tea after which they then watered and fed the animals. They moved the horses from the barn and walked them around and were pleased to see that they were relaxed and calm. The rams were tied to the wagon and were laying down with the dogs alongside them. The horses were then hobbled and left to wander. They all ate and drank normally, they were fit to travel. Michael decided to stay another day and to leave early in the morning. He, Stan and Tabu needed a good day's rest to be ready for the unknown.

Old Bill wanted a watchman to walk around all the buildings two or three times each hour and to keep their eye open for smoke or visible fire. Michael volunteered to do the first few hours; he would be able to get a good night's uninterrupted sleep afterwards. The night was full of stars with a half moon and was very quiet. The air was still smoky but it was cool and still. He could still see smoke clouds in the distance and he wondered if the wind was of concern in the vicinity of where the fire now was.

His few hours on watch were uneventful and at its end he went and shook the next watchman who was fast asleep. He staggered to his feet and thanked Michael, and wandered down towards the inn for his few hours of 'watch keeping'.

The wagon was next to the big barn. Michael decided to sleep under it with the dogs tied to the wheel. He soon dropped into a deep slumber only to be woken by the frantic barking of the dogs.

He awoke through a haze of weariness to smell smoke. Smoke! Where! He saw that the big barn had smoke coming from the open loft door where there had been a lookout. Exactly as the timber cutter said — Watch for smoke. The settlement was now wide awake the dogs had woken everyone with their loud barking.

Old Bill ran up and asked Michael if he knew where the smoke was coming from. He pointed to the smoke coming from the barn's loft door.

Two ladders were soon placed below the opening to the loft. Jamie and a mate dashed up the ladders and vanished inside.

Jamie appeared, he threw down a smoldering bale of hay to the ground and then another, yelling. 'Buckets of water, quickly.' A bucket brigade was formed and the fire was soon extinguished. It was a close call as barns are notorious for fires, particularly in the lofts.

Old Bill's hackles were up, he was after blood. He looked around at everyone and no one.

'Who was the watchman? How did you miss the fire?' yelled Bill.

A young timber cutter stepped forward saying. 'It was me. I fell asleep. I'm sorry.'

Old Bill looked at him for a long time and then slowly walked away. He realised that the youth was truly sorry and he knew the boy had done a good job of clearing the river bank of the trees. Jamie walked over to the distraught youth and said. 'There was no damage done, we caught it in time. Dad will get over it.'

As we stood around feeling much relieved, Jamie said to no one in particular but really to everyone 'We should have thought to close the loft door after the fire was over. That's where the ember entered. There were only two smoldering bales but others were scorched. We can relax now'

Old Bill's voice bellowed. 'No, you bloody can't, I'll keep watch myself until dawn. The rest of you go back to bed. I'll stay up myself.' He then stomped off into night. Later that night he put out a small smolder in a tussock, but that was the last incident.

The next morning, they all took the opportunity to walk around the burnt areas. The fire break outer edge clearly defined the fire limit. Blackened grass neatly bordered the ploughed area. The river bank foliage further up the river was still showing wisps of smoke but was of no concern. Some of the trees felled by the timber cutters would need to be cleared as they were blocking the river and would cause further problems when the heavy winter rains would wash down more fallen trees from up stream. The head timber cutter promised the small community that he to return within the month and clear the debris.

Michael walked further up river to see the remains of the burnt trees. He was surprised to see some green leaves still on top of the upper small branches of trees that had been on fire. The bark had peeled from most of the trees with some of the trees showing the white inner wood.

He had seen bush fire damage before and yet within three months the burnt paddocks, and with a little rain, this same ground would have a healthy cover of greenery, either of grass or shrub shoots. He guessed old Bill's property would fare the same.

He strolled around the buildings and could see no major

damage from the bushfire. Only a scorch mark here and there. Other than that, the settlement looked no different from any other settlement. It was neat and tidy, no doubt the clean-up helped improve its appearance. A few gigs, wagons and horses at the hitching rail completed the rural picture together with the river background. After the few days of drama, this was the picture Michael would remember in years to come whenever the subject of bushfire was raised.

It was time to go. The animals had been fed, the horses harnessed and the wagon loaded. The settlement residents, farmers and timber cutters were all there to farewell them. Handshakes and some hugs for himself and Stan. The women had made some scones and cakes for their journey. They would be a pleasant change from their normal boring meals.

After the fire had passed by, Tabu had returned to the wagon to feed the animals but he had not been forgotten. Several of the men who had had previous dealings with aboriginal stockmen, shook his hand saying 'Thanks.' The other men and women, who had not met an aborigine before stood back and just nodded to him. It's doubtful if he saw the nods. Generally, Tabu avoided eye contact, as did most aborigines.

Stan and Tabu had moved the sheep from the pens and the dogs started moving them from the settlement. Michael slapped the reins on the wagon horse's flank, they took up the slack and started plodding out heading north. The spare horse was tied to rear of the wagon, with Tabu and Stan riding alongside the sheep. Michael waved back several times and then turned and looked forward — to what? The bushfire had cost Michael four days. He would be late for his rendezvous in Echuca.

The wind was blowing from the north. The grass was a light brown and the ground parched. Dust was everywhere. It got into one's eyes, nose and throat. Smoke from several other grass fires could be seen in the distance and would be a worry for them for the next few days. They would need to stay alert both night and day watching for wind changes. They had been travelling for two days now without water for the sheep and only had a limited water supply for themselves, the horses and the dogs. Michael guessed that there had been no rainfall for a month or two and the water holes were now dry.

Tabu pointed to a line of green trees in the distance. Michael nodded; he knew that trees like these would be on the banks of a river or at least a big creek. Hopefully there would be water and that they would all be drinking tonight.

They were right. It was a small river with flowing water. The river water was welcomed by the drovers and the animals. It was both clear and cool. The men sat in the water and poured water from their hats over their heads. The animals each found an area at the river to slate their thirst.

They camped there that night and headed out the next morning with their water casks full. Fortunately, the river was very shallow and flowing slowly and was easy for the sheep to walk across.

Normally Michael would expect to get sufficient water for the sheep at any river or billabong but in these hot months and because he was in unfamiliar territory he had to plan ahead. He urgently needed to locate another water source within two or three days of droving after crossing this river. He sent Tabu ahead to find such a supply.

The area Michael was now in had not been mapped and only the drovers who had come north earlier had acquired any local knowledge of water availability. He knew that there were flocks already grazing near the Murray River, so he had presumed that water was somewhere on this track — all he needed was some luck and good bush skills — with Tabu, he had the bush skills.

Daily Michael was learning from him. The tracks of previous flocks and drovers were still obvious in the area. The virgin tufts had been trodden on by thousands of sheep sharp hooves. It was logical to follow them and would save them considerable time looking for a new way through the dense shrub land which occurred often.

The sparse grass lands had gradually changed colour, from the dry light brown to a light green colour, as the flock plodded north. Soon they were among the trees. They continued to follow wheel ruts through the scattered trees and where the grass had been trampled by at least one flock of sheep and one herd of cattle. Animal dung was frequent and appeared to be only a few weeks old. Michael would follow this track. He would like to have explored, looking for an alternative route, but he did not have the time. Tabu returned within two days with news that there was ample water within a day or so droving and more good water within three days droving.

The sheep needed to be kept bunched as they were prone to wandering in the shrub country. The trees were not easy to negotiate. The saplings on the trees continually slapped the drovers in the face. Finding a suitable camping place was difficult, they pushed on until darkness had fallen and then they decided to sleep in the wagon. Michael was frightened of snakes. They rarely saw one as the noise of the droving made the snakes move away from them. But they each needed to be alert and watchful.

Eventually they moved into grasslands again and headed to another tree line where Tabu said there was water. The sun was hot and the air dry. The animals were listless and Michael felt exhausted due to the persistent heat. Finally, on the second day, just before sunset they were at the river bank.

The sheep were pushing and bumping into each other as

they surged forward to drink the fresh clear river water. It had a large shallow open bank which allowed each of the sheep to drink their fill.

Michael's horse stood up to its belly in the river drinking, while he filled his hat with water alternately drinking some of the water and then pouring the remainder over his head. Stan and Tabu were sitting in the water and drinking. They decided to stay a day here and rest.

They were making good time but they would still not be in Echuca on the previously arranged date. In the distance, the shimmering reflection from buildings roofs began to appear.

Slowly they began to take shape, several large sheds and two houses. There was extensive fencing where cattle, a few horses and sheep were grazing. Windmill fans squeaked while raising and lowering their pump shafts and lifting bore water into an open water trough. A dot on the horizon soon became a horseman. He was long and lean and sat his horse comfortably. You could see he was an experienced horseman.

He nodded to Michael and said 'G'day, where're you from?'

Michael answered. 'We left Kyneton over two weeks ago, we're heading to Echuca.'

The horse man nodded saying. 'My name's Jim Forest. You're welcome to stay awhile. My wife would appreciate some visitors. We have plenty of accommodation in shearers' quarters.'

'Thanks, it would be nice to sleep in a bed for a change.' He pointed 'That's Stan and Tabu and I'm Michael Somerset.' said Michael, nodding at each in turn. 'Can I yard my sheep?'

'Yes, use the big yard on your left next to the smaller house and you can bunk in that house. Come up to the big house when you've settled in. My wife's name is June'. He waved and then rode off.

Stan declined the offer to go to the big house, he was rather a shy person, and Tabu as usual had vanished, so only Michael dined with Jim and June. It was a pleasant evening. They had a game of cards while the Forest's talked of their previous life in Cumberland.

Their parents had been farmers near Carlisle. They missed the old country but not its weather. They preferred the other extreme — plenty of sun. Their three children were now adults and had their own farms all within an hour's ride from here. They were happy with their lot.

At day-break they were all up and about. The dogs and horses had been feed and the wagon hitched. The horses were in good condition and their shoes were still intact. Breakfast was more than ample. Michael didn't think he would need any lunch today. A few quick 'thanks and farewells', Michael and his team were on the track again.

The previous night Jim had commented that a neighbour of his had sheep ready to be shorn and he was having trouble getting shearers.

Michael mentioned this to Stan, who said he was happy to do some shearing. They could always do with some extra money, it all added up, particularly for Michael, if he was going to buy some more land. It was agreed that they would go to the farm and offer their services.

Michael rode on ahead to met with the farmer. He was happy to offer Michael the job at the going rate per hundred. The farm had 500 sheep with fleeces that were clean and free of burrs and twigs.

It would be a quick and easy task. Michael was happy to have some small shearing jobs, as the time spent shearing would also allow his sheep to have extra feed and keep their condition. He accepted two other shearing jobs before reaching Echuca. He knew he was late, so why worry! What's another day or another week!

At one of the shearing sheds, there was another shearing contractor with three shearers and a roustabout. Both teams got on well together until one shearer complained that he had had money and a watch taken from his clothes when he was he was bathing in the dam. Suspicion fell on everyone and the friendly mood in the shed changed dramatically. The property owner quickly solved the problem. The next morning, he walked into the men's sleeping quarters and asked everyone to empty out their swags and pockets.

One shearer showed some reluctance and the owner then levelled a shotgun at him and ordered him to empty his pockets or he would tie him up until a Constable arrived. This particular shearer had the stolen watch in his money belt. He was thrown into the dam, painted with green sheep brand dye including his hair, then put on his horse and sent on his way without pay. This was typical of Australian 'Bush Justice'.

The town of Echuca finally appeared on the horizon. It was situated on the banks of the Murray River, which originated from the high country in the New South Wales/Victorian eastern ranges and continued its long meandering journey over to the border of South Australia and down to the coast.

Michael could see two paddle boats chugging along the fast-flowing Murray River waters. One was hauling large logs and the other following, seemingly top heavy with large wool bales stacked on its upper deck. They sat on their horses looking at the river waters and the gum trees with sunshine filtering through their leafy branches. It was pleasant sight to be enjoyed after their travels.

Echuca's port looked busy with wagons and drays moving here and there and people milling around the many stores along the river bank. They would soon arrive at the town centre. Michael sent Stan on ahead to locate some sheep pens, while

Tabu and he stopped about a mile from the town and waiting for him to return. An hour or so later, Stan returned shouting and waving them to start moving the sheep. He had located the public pens that were next to the Victorian Customs House at the river border crossing to New South Wales.

As they herded the sheep into the pens, several Custom Officers walked over.

They waited for Michael to dismount before speaking.

The senior Officer nodded and said 'Where might you be from Sir?'

'I'm from Kyneton, I'm Michael Somerset,' replied Michael.

The other Custom Officers were looking at the ewes and the rams.

'Is this your brand, Mr Somerset?' he was asked.

'Yes, it is,' said Michael. His brand was a — three teethed key.

'Are you selling them?' the Officer continued.

Michael sensed an attitude. He said 'Yes.'

'There may be a tax to be paid on each head.' There was no friendliness in his tone.

Michael said nothing for a few seconds.

'Oh, that's the first I've heard of that.'

'Well, Mr. Somerset, that's the rule and it must be paid before you go any further.'

Michael answered. 'Well, can I leave them here for a day or so?'

The Officer looked at Michael and nodded. 'Yes, but don't try to move them or there will be trouble for you.'

Michael walked away leading his horse. Tabu and Stan were standing nearby and listening.

Michael was surprised to hear of the tax, they were still in Victoria and he had made no mention of crossing the border into New South Wales. It was agreed that they would camp on the river bank not far from the crossing.

Michael decided to see if he could contact Mr. Rooke. He rode down the main street and stopped outside the largest Stock Agent, dismounting he entered and asked the receptionist if he could speak to one of the agents, as he wished to locate a Mr. Rooke.

She looked at him and asked 'Would you be Mr. Somerset Sir?'

Surprised, Michael said 'Yes, I am.'

The receptionist turned to some mail pigeon holes in the wall and removed an envelope and handed it to him. 'We have been expecting you. Mr. Rooke said to give you this letter. The directions to his property are enclosed.'

Michael thanked her and went to a seat outside the main door, sat down and opened the letter. It was a letter of welcome and requested Michael to 'Cross the river at the town border crossing and proceed north on the main road for roughly two miles to the first road on the west side of the main road, turn left and follow this road for another mile and you will see the name 'Rooke's Rest' on the front gate. The farmhouse can be seen from the gate.'

He found Stan and Tabu lying half asleep near the wagon. As it was still daylight and he guessed that the ride to 'Rooke's Rest' would only take half an hour or so, Michael decided that he would go there now. He then turned his horse and went back to cross the bridge.

The Custom Officer waved him to stop and asked 'Where are you off to?'

Michael said 'Going to see a friend, I'll be back by morning. Why do you want to know?'

The Officer stared at him for a second then walked away.

The ride to Mr Rooke's was quicker than Michael expected. As he rode up the lane to the farm house, he was greeted by two yapping dogs and a thick set man on a pony who waved to him and asked 'And who might you be young fellow?'

Michael smiling answered. 'I might be Michael Somerset from Kyneton and I presume you are Hedley Rooke?'

Hedley laughed and said 'Follow me to the house.' They dismounted, tied their horses to the rail alongside the veranda and Michael followed him into the house.

'Welcome, I was wondering where you were,' queried Hedley.

'Yes, we had a few problems during the droving.' Michael gave Hedley a quick version of the reason for their delayed arrival.

He did not mention the shearing he had done on the way. He concluded by advising that all of the sheep were in good condition and were being held at the public pens adjacent the Customs House.

Hedley interjected asking 'Did you have any trouble with the Custom Officers?'

Michael said 'Well now that you mention it, they told me of a tax for each head of sheep, even though I had not mentioned to them that they were coming to New South Wales.'

Hedley said 'I would expect that you will get an unofficial visit from a middleman who will offer you a way around having to pay all of the tax, of course he will expect to receive remuneration from you. We believe the Senior Customs Officer is behind the scheme but he hasn't been caught yet. I'm a Justice of the Peace and I know that the Police have been monitoring this problem for a while.'

Michael thought for a moment and said 'Have you considered using marked bank notes. These are paid by the stockman to the middle man and with any luck — he will pay the Senior Customs Officer his share with some of the marked notes. When he tries to cash them, Bingo! You have your culprit. I know it sounds simple but I recently read of a story in London where it was tried and it worked.'

Hedley smiled and said 'What a capital idea. I have fifty

cattle coming over the border next week. I'll talk to the Police in Echuca about your idea and see if they can agree that we try your idea with the head stockman of the herd. He will not be known here.'

Michael nodded saying 'My small flock will probably be of no interest to their theft scheme. I'd like to bring them to you tomorrow.' Michael paused. 'While I'm in the district I want to explore land along the Murray River to the east around Tongala and Moira and I would like to start as soon as possible.'

Hedley nodded agreement and stood up. 'I'll organise a bank draft for you tomorrow at noon. You can put the sheep in the pens near my main gate. Well, until tomorrow goodbye.'

Michael followed him to the horses. He mounted his horse and with a quick wave went back to riverside camp.

The three of them rose early, had breakfast and packed the wagon. They did not receive a visit from a middleman during the night. Michael was right. Their flock was too small to be of any fraudulent monetary interest.

The Customs Officer came to Michael and told him the tax. Michael did not argue he paid and they then headed the sheep and the wagon north to Hedley's farm. At noon Hedley handed Michael his Bank Draft.

Michael banked the draft and then paid Stan his wages from the money he had collected from his shearing contracts. Stan had decided to stay in Echuca and seek work on the river boats. A quick farewell and he walked into to town.

Michael was eager to explore the land east of Echuca and arranged to leave the wagon and the two dogs at Rooke's farm. Tabu and he needed to travel light through the little-known country district. A wagon would slow them down, so they decided to take the two horses as pack horses. Michael and Tabu loaded the pack horses with flour, tea, salt, meat, camping gear and some tools. They carried their rifles and revolvers with them in their saddle holsters. They headed out of town and were soon in bush lands. Generally, they followed the direction of the Murray River to the east and then to the north but they did not follow every twist and turn of its course which it did every few miles. The country was predominately grassland with small forests of trees and dense shrub along the steep river banks.

At times, they found other tracks of horses and sometimes saw aborigines in the distance and the smoke from their fires. They probably knew Michael and Tabu were close but the aborigines showed no interest in them.

They only came on one small farm, with a few sheep and two horses. The settler looked an unsavoury character with a long dirty beard, dressed in rags and carrying a long barrel single shot 'cap and ball' rifle. They weren't invited 'to stop and have a cuppa' not that they would have accepted his invitation. His mangy dog looked cleaner. The settler was sullen and definitely did not welcome company. His attitude was typical of an ex-convict.

His sheep were unbranded so maybe he was inclined to rustle them from over the river or perhaps he was evading the law for other reasons. The sharp hooves of his sheep had worn a deep muddy track, coming from the direction of the river.

Michael and Tabu rode for a further ten days, taking their time exploring the countryside before reaching Moira. They then crossed the river and followed it for five days before turning back. They tracked back to Tongala then turned west and followed the Goulburn River back to Echuca. The land was similar with flat grasslands and huge river gums trees. These trees had large branches with unique smelling leaves. Some trees had their roots exposed due to the erosion of the root soil, due to the power of the high spring flood waters coming down from the mountain range in the east.

Michael had been most impressed with the country they had covered. He could see that it had enormous potential for both grazing and farming. He would come back one day and hopefully be able to claim a river frontage area for himself. They had now been exploring for nearly four weeks. He began to look forward to returning home.

He and Tabu had encounted a few aboriginal tribes and had found them to be wary but not prone to being aggressive. They were able to converse but with difficulty. Fortunately, some aborigines had worked on cattle or sheep stations and they helped answer most of Michael's questions.

When they returned to Echuca they went back to Rooke's farm. Hedley saw them coming and walked up the lane to meet them. He greeted them 'How was your trip? You look tired. Come in and have a meal.'

Michael dismounted and they shook hands and he answered. 'Yes, it was a tiring trip but it was well worth the effort.'

He handed the reins of his horse to Tabu and followed Hedley into the farm house. He knew Tabu would tend the horses and find himself a spot to rest and he had food in his saddle bags. After drinking a cup of welcomed tea, Michael spoke of their travels. He described the countryside, the land, foliage, flora and fauna and the aborigines. He said he may return to the Goulburn river area and attempt to acquire land north of the river. It was indeed a very fertile area. Although they didn't see any during their travels, Michael knew that the most of the area south of the river was controlled by Squatters at the moment, so it could be difficult to settle there until the two Governments decided how their State lands were to be allotted.

Hedley asked several questions regarding the aborigines, their fearsome reputation and how trustworthy would they be to employ.

Michael replied 'Their reputation is not as bad as you may think and yes, they can be employed, look at Tabu. He's excellent, although he is from a southern tribe, we had no trouble with your river tribes.' Hedley nodded as he listened.

Hedley then said 'By the way your idea regarding the Customs swindle worked. The Head stockman, of that large flock that we spoke of, paid the middleman with marked pound notes. A week later the Senior Customs Officer tended one of the one pound notes to the Echuca Bank of New South Wales.'

He continued 'The teller had been alerted and identified the number immediately. He feigned a temporary indisposition and excused himself. He went to the Manager and told him. The manager ran out of the back door to the Police station, which was only three buildings from the Bank. The Police walked through the front door of the Bank and immediately challenged him as to where had he obtained the marked one pound note.'

Hedley paused 'He tried to lie by saying he had had the one pound note for over a month and had received it as salary. When he was advised that the one pound note was listed a week ago by the Bank with its number being recorded by the Police at that time, he sat down and confessed. It appeared another Officer and himself were the main ones involved in the deception.'

Michael said 'Excellent, what a good result!'

The Customs Officers were altering the official head count of the stock and only charging 50% of the correct tax while the middle man collected 25% of the tax during his nightly visits to the head drovers and then gave half of it to the two Custom Officers.

Hedley welcomed Michael's company and persuaded him to stay a few days before heading home. Michael accepted the invitation, he enjoyed two days sleeping in a real bed and having farm cooked meals. On the third day feeling fully rested, he loaded the wagon, and with Tabu, they watered and feed the horses and the dogs and made ready to head south. After a large breakfast, he walked to the wagon, accompanied by Hedley.

Michael shook his hand and thanked him for his kindness, saying 'I hope my sheep will give you a good new flock, perhaps we'll meet again. Goodbye.'

He climbed into the wagon with Tabu, and with a shake of the reins, the horse started to trot down the lane towards Echuca. The other horses were tied to the wagon's tailgate with the dogs running alongside yelping. Michael would give them a short run before lifting them into the wagon. He turned and waved to Hedley. He was happy — he was now heading home.

CHAPTER THREE

The Voyage

Major John Hall led a detachment of soldiers from the local Regiment down the main street of Kyneton. They were heading back to their barracks. It had been a long and hot day so he decided to stop at the water trough for the horses to drink. The detachment had escorted a Gold consignment from Heathcote, which they had just handed over to another Gold escort travelling to Melbourne.

Whilst watering his horse at the water trough, John happened to glance at the Post Office notice board and saw an advertisement with a listing of ships sailing dates to Liverpool. For some time now he had been thinking of his family in Cumberland, particularly of his father who was now in his advanced years and was becoming infirm. He had not been back to the family home in England, for over seven years. Also, his brother in law, Michael Somerset, had raised the subject of how their wool was being sold to the Manchester Mills. This would be a chance to have direct negotiations with the Mills owners and perhaps reduce their broker's charges.

That evening John sat with his wife Maeve, and asked her thoughts about them visiting his family home. She thought for a few moments and said then simply 'Why not?'

The next day John also pondered -why not! He had a successful military career and had risen through the ranks to a senior position. He was a successful farmer and had established himself as a pillar of the local society. Why not indeed!

He immediately wrote to his Commanding Officer requesting six months leave of absence to visit his family in England.

He had not taken any extended Military leave for five years. The extended leave time was not an unusual request for a senior Government Officer, due to the time required to travel to England and return. He was on good terms with the Commandant and was pleased to receive approval within the week. It was subject to him performing a formal handover with the relieving officer, who would arrive within the week. The handover was duly carried out within four days.

John could now arrange his passage to England. Connor his farm hand, was capable of running the farm and the livestock, and his bank manager would see that the finances were kept in order. He then had a meeting with Michael regarding the brokerage and sale of their wool to the Manchester Mills and they had decided how he would approach the issue. Obviously removing any brokerage charges would be a cost saving for both of them and perhaps others in the district.

However, whenever he approached Maeve about them travelling together, she would emphatically say, 'No!'

She said 'We have two young boys and my father is ailing as you know and it is my responsibility to tend to each of them. I have my father and brother here but you don't. You must go, as time waits for no one. You've raised the subject, now you must go or you may regret it in the years to come.'

As much as John tried to get Maeve to come with him, it was difficult to argue with her logic. So, he decided to go alone and began to finalise his local arrangements.

He could still remember how cold the English country side could be so he packed some heavy outer clothing and on the spur of the moment included his revolver, together with some books on the Colonies and a few local souvenirs.

John knew that he would miss Maeve's company, but after some tearful farewells and many good wishes, John took the morning coach to Melbourne to book his passage. He was to sail in three days' time; this would give him sufficient time to make arrangements with his Melbourne bank, his stock agent and to meet with some Melbourne friends for a farewell dinner or two.

The next few days were somewhat hectic but enjoyable and he was becoming excited at the prospect of seeing his family after all these years. Questions kept popping into his mind. How much had they changed? Was the farm different? Had the English weather improved? He doubted it. Were any of his friends still in the district? Yes, he was excited. He was actually returning to his original home after all of these years in Victoria — albeit only for a visit. Sailing day soon arrived.

As the S.S. Ingleton ship cleared the Heads on the high tide, John stood at the stern on the pitching deck watching the land disappear in the mist. Abeam there were many other vessels lining up to enter Port Phillip Bay. Melbourne was now an important destination with its imports and exports and yet it was only around two decades since it had been settled. He strongly believed it was the country of the future and he was glad he had made the decision to make his home here in the Antipodes.

A week after John left, Maeve received an official letter from a Melbourne lawyer. The letter alleged that a particular Company held the water rights to his property and several others in the district and that no fees had been paid to the Company for the last five years and as such compensation would be required. Maeve immediately contacted the family Kyneton lawyer who advised her that he was already investigating these allegations on behalf of some of the other local farmers.

The water rights allegation sent a shiver down the spine of residents throughout the entire district. The allegation stated that the water titles covered areas within specific geographical co-ordinates and Maeve's lawyer confirmed that the co-ordinates covered their property. Maeve asked the lawyer if he could delay any action until John returned. The lawyer said the best that he could do was to request a 'Stay of Proceedings' on any action, until they had obtained copies of all of the associated documents of the Water Titles.

Within a week, Maeve received a letter from their lawyer who said that copies of the documents were held in the Echuca Lands Office. He asked if she could send someone to ride there and collect the copies and when they arrived, if they could have a district meeting and decide what to do next.

Maeve immediately sent Connor and Michael sending Tabu to accompany him on the journey to Echuca. Connor arrived back within the week with several rolls of large documents and immediately took them to their Kyneton lawyer. Four days later the lawyer convened a meeting with twenty local farmers and their families. The mood at the meeting was sombre, they all feared the worst. The lawyer ponderously unrolled the large sheets of documents and starting to read, with the mood of the group becoming worse. When he stopped, he sat down without saying a word. Maeve arranged tea. No one spoke.

Connor was standing by the titles and was looking intently at the small print at the bottom corner of one particular title.

William Eden asked. 'What are you so interested in?'

Connor said 'This document was signed in Sydney when this area was named the District of Port Phillip and it was part of the Colony of New South Wales?'

William nodded 'Yes and?'

The lawyer walked quickly to the table, put on his glasses and looked closely at the wording.

'Yes,' he said. 'But this is the Colony of Victoria now, not the Colony of New South Wales!'

He looked up and stated. 'I don't believe these documents are now valid. The Laws of the Colony of New South Wales no longer apply to the former Port Phillip District.' The room was silent, then after a short pause, they all realised the implication of what had been said, the room was suddenly full of talk and hope.

The lawyer took the coach to Melbourne the next morning, loaded with his documents. Three weeks later he wrote to each affected farmer and advised them that the allegations were null and void. It appeared that this ploy had been tried in Gippsland several months before and had nearly been successful. John would be pleased how Maeve had handled the situation — so was Maeve!

The S.S. Ingleton continued to sail east with the strong westerly winds at her stern. This initial leg would be the longest, Melbourne to Montevideo, the next to Rio de Janiero and finally to their destination of Liverpool.

The ship was under command of Captain William Badger and it carried twenty passengers in separate cabins and a cargo of wool destined for the spinning mills of Manchester. Wool from the Colonies was now in demand in both the British Isles and Europe. Australian merino wool had been identified as one of the finest in the world, having being introduced in the Colony of New South Wales from South Africa in the early 1800's. These sheep were hardy and handled the harsh Australian climate with ease.

Captain Badger was an experienced old salt, who had risen from a cabin boy to a master mariner in a career of over thirty years. He soon had the ship clipping along at a smart pace. The seas were slightly 'choppy', the majority of the time the bow was under a light spray of eye-stinging salt water with very few passengers venturing onto the deck. The spray not only stung their face and eyes but it quickly drenched their clothes and sometimes painfully chaffed the skin.

John read and wrote, played solo, anything to help pass the time. He even made a list of questions to ask his family. He wrote down all the names of his school friends that he could remember. He wondered — where were they now? Time rolled on ever so slowly.

During an evening dinner chaired by the Captain, he casually remarked to the passengers. 'We will soon have a change in the weather and you will start feeling the ship roll and pitch more than usual, as we enter the seas rounding Cape Horn, the southern tip of South America. This unpleasant turbulence will be felt for around a week or so. However, once around the Horn, the seas would abate and the voyage to the north will be comfortable and you will be able to enjoy some deck time.' The table talk became somewhat nervous in anticipation of the coming sailing conditions.

John had experienced rough seas on his trip to Victoria and he hadn't forgotten the lessons learnt. He packed his baggage and wedged them in the space between the bulkhead and the bunk side. The port hole had proven to be water tight since he had left Melbourne. He hadn't opened it yet and had no plans to do it now.

He decided to chance a visit on deck. He borrowed an oilskin cape from a sailor and ventured onto the deck while holding onto a guard rail. He could see land in the distance off the port bow, and that the sea had white caps as far as the eye could see. Mist shrouded the landmass peaks, and the scene over the bow was gloomy and dark. It looked ominous. He would be glad when they were in the South Atlantic Ocean.

Whistles sounded and the megaphone called the duty watch to batten down the hatches, secure the ropes and loose deck cargo and then to man their stations. The time was nigh, although the next three hours were relatively quiet. The wind was steady and seas moderate. The Captain not only had his experience but he also had a barometer to assist him — it was starting to fall. The weather would change within the next two hours, with not only the seas around the horn expected to be rough but also heavy rain and gusting winds were anticipated.

The seas churned with white caps everywhere. The first wind was vicious and sudden. The ship heeled and then tossed like a bucking horse. The sea troughs were short and steep and seas poured over the ship and out under the guard rails. The passengers were already in their cabins and were lying flat on their bunks holding on to the sides, hoping not to be thrown about or even out of their bunks. The ship held its head and ploughed on into the seas. The sails had been reefed with only about a fifth of available sail now being used. The sea anchor was ready but hopefully no emergency would arise that would require its use.

The Captain stayed in the wheelhouse and would be there for as long as possible. Only extreme lack of sleep would drive him to his cabin, when the First Mate would take over command. The Captain remained in the wheel house for sixteen hours a day and the First Mate eight hours. The Captain did this for three days.

The ship thrashed though the seas. Only one incident caused concern, a beam-on rogue wave stove in a plank at the waterline on the port side. The shipwrights soon installed a plank inside the damaged area. The bilge water pumps were manned and the crew soon had the bilge empty of excessive water. The bilge always had some water in it. One of the shipwrights was badly bruised when he thrown off his feet onto a wooden beam by the ship's violent pitching.

The heavy seas continued for two more days before the passengers were able to have a cooked meal. After five days, the ship turned north east into the South Atlantic Ocean. John and most of the other passengers were now able to enjoy stretching their legs and breathing fresh air again. The hatches were opened to allow sea air to be circulated throughout the ship's hull.

When he met his fellow passengers at dinner the first night after rounding the Horn, he was surprised to see that several were suffering broken bones. Three of them had been thrown from their bunks and one had his sea trunk fall on him when he was opening it for some clothing. The Doctor had been kept busy tending these injured passengers and some bruised crew members. The Captain conversed with the passengers and stated that apart from the damaged plank, the ship's only losses or damages were to some galley equipment, although most galley equipment was made of metal or wood.

The remainder of the voyage passed quickly. John wasn't interested in going ashore at Montevideo. It was raining with a cold wind blowing and with this dismal weather, the city appeared uninviting. The ship took on water and some fresh food and sailed on the next tide.

The ship's arrival at Rio De Janiero was very different. It was a warm sunny day with a cloudless sky. Sugarloaf Mountain towered majestically behind the city and its long wide beach beckoned to be visited. He and a fellow passenger hired a gig and toured the along the foreshore road. He bought a few souvenirs and had lunch opposite the beach. It was good to be ashore even if it could only be for a few hours. As they did in Montevideo, they sailed on the next tide, bound for Liverpool. After several more days of sailing, the mood on the ship became one of anticipation. They were nearing the end of their long voyage.

When John first felt the coldness of the Irish Sea he knew he would soon be home. The coast of England was off the starboard beam, he was pleasantly surprised that he was becoming excited at seeing land.

He was a mature man who should be able to control his emotions or should he? His parents did not expect him home. What would they be like after these seven years?

They had corresponded regularly but an answer to a letter could take three or four months. Much could happen in four months. They would still have a lot to talk about, not only about his family but also Michael's. Although his family had only meet Maeve once, his family enquired of her in each letter.

The voyage had taken seven weeks. At the final dinner with Captain Badger, prior to arriving in Liverpool, he chanced to comment he would be sailing back to Melbourne in a month's time. John had planned to stay about a month.

The Captain said 'I'm here for a month as the ship needs some work. If you sail back with me I will see that you have my best cabin'.

John laughed and replied. 'I accept your offer and will return to Melbourne on the S.S. Ingleton.'

The ship docked early morning with custom clearance being only a formality. The farewells were brief and soon completed with the ship being emptied of both passengers and cargo within three hours. John went to a coach office and after a wait of two hours, he was off to Penrith. The English countryside was lush and green and with the long summer evenings and daylight lasting until ten pm, it wasn't difficult to remain awake and enjoy the scenery. It was a pleasant change from the voyage.

After a few changes of horses, the coach eventually reached a small wayside inn half way to Penrith. He decided to remain the night to ensure he would feel fresh when he arrived home tomorrow. After a good sleep, he embarked on the first morning coach destined for Penrith. The views from the coach had now become monotonous and John began to doze between horse changes. He arrived at Penrith mid-afternoon and with the extra hours of daylight available he decided to hire a horse and gig and drive home — a two hour trip.

He approached 'Brackenshire', the principal family farm, down a road leading directly to its entrance. He could still read the faded name 'Brackenshire' over the gateway even though it was nearly overgrown by the hedges. Although the hedge was well trimmed, its size now made it more imposing than he remembered. The long carriageway leading to the farm house had small English box hedges lining either side. These were neatly trimmed to around three feet in height.

The paddocks either side of the carriageway had cattle grazing. Some lifted their heads while chewing their cud, looked vacantly at him as he rode by and then showing no further interest, they went back to grazing. As he approached the house he felt an emotion grow in him that he had not felt before. He was back in his father's house, where he had grown up.

He reined to stop the horse, in front of the main door and sat looking at a light in the front window. He could see people moving around inside. He wondered who they might be. He had a lump in his throat.

The first person to see him was Ann, the maid who was walking from the laundry. She stopped and looked at him twice and then putting her hand to her mouth she exclaimed. 'Mr. John, is that you?'

John dismounted, tied the horse to a rail and answered laughingly. 'Yes, it's me.'

A voice behind him said. 'No! No! It can't be. I don't believe it, you are home.' It was his sister Maryanne.

John turned and opened his arms to hug his crying sister. The excited noise made by the two women was heard inside the house. His mother and father came out to see what all the commotion was about.

Their eyes lit up when they saw it was John. They stood there for a moment or two and then smilingly, they stepped forward and hugged in a group.

His mother kept saying 'John, John.' His father then shook his hand without speaking. John was surprised to see his father show emotion. His mother saying. 'Come inside! Oh, it's wonderful to see you again.'

John's mother led them into the drawing room, where they placed their chairs into a circle. His father spoke first. 'I could not have wanted for a better surprise than this.' He saw the gig and said. 'Don't worry about the horse and gig. I'll have Jack return it tomorrow.'

His sister chipped in. 'Where do we start? You have lots to tell us. Start with your life in the colonies? How is Maeve?'

John laughed putting his hand up and saying 'Slow down! I'm home for a month, I have questions too.'

His father put up his hand and nodded saying 'You should start first as you will have stories to tell us of which we have no idea, we will only be updating you on local issues.'

John nodded in agreement thinking, where do I start? Firstly, he handed over the books and souvenirs he had brought with him, which delighted them all. John then sat back in his chair and cast his mind back to the day he left Liverpool. He started to talk. His family sat quietly listening to his every word. The only interruption was when Ann advised that supper was ready to be served.

As they dined John began talking again. He related his sea voyage, losing the mast in the stormy weather, hitting a whale and diverting to Mauritius, then joining the Victorian Militia and his clash with the bushrangers, his farming endeavours, the arrival of Maeve, their marriage and the locating of Michael, Maeve's brother. Much of what he said had been written and advised previously in his letters. He spoke for over an hour answering a few questions.

He noticed that his mother looked weary. He suggested that they should all retire and talk again tomorrow. They agreed and after a few kisses and a firm hand shake from his father, John and his family retired early for the night.

The next morning John rose at day break. After an early breakfast, he decided to walk around the farm buildings and refresh his memory. He walked to the stables and then to the horse paddocks and was surprised to see his old horse Duke. He was looking very fit with a lovely shiny black coat. He was now eleven years old and still stood straight and tall. The horse walked to the paddock fence and stood still, John walked slowly to him and then stroked his nose. Duke stood placidly — did he remember John? The horse soon became bored and wandered off to his water trough.

Out of the corner of his eye, he spotted a person exiting the main barn, he recognised his walk. It was Jack Keane the farm manager. He walked over to him and said 'Good morning Jack.'

Jack turned and looked at John with surprise and said 'Where did you spring from? I didn't know you were coming home.' Shaking John's hand, he continued. 'The colonies are treating you well, you look hale and hearty.'

John responded 'After seven years away, I thought it was time to return and see the family and Yes, I'm now a colonial. I love the country and its lifestyle, its weather is much more pleasant with plenty of sunshine.'

Jack nodded. 'You're obviously happy, I'm pleased for you. The farm has had some changes, let me show you around.'

Jack led John to the door of the main barn and pointed to the false ceiling which had been added to store fodder for the livestock in the winter months. Several more stalls had been added. Some stalls were exclusive for Maryanne's horses which she had bred and trained for County equestrian events. A new tack room completed the additions. They then walked to a new building. Jack explained that John's father had decided several years ago to have his own slaughter room and hire the local butcher when needed. It had proved to be profitable as he also hired the facility to other local farmers for them to do their slaughtering. It was a 'win-win' business idea.

Jack walked to the paddock in front of the main barn and pointed to the sheep grazing in the distance. He said 'As you know, this is the highest point of the farm and naturally the best drained paddock. Its fifty acres, well grassed, and can carry four sheep to the acre so we rarely need dry fodder.' Jack paused. 'We decided to concentrate on wool rather than meat. The Manchester mills cannot get enough wool. We have the next grazing paddock lying fallow.'

John answered. 'Yes, I'm aware of the Manchester mills need for wool, I breed Merino sheep and I believe they are one of the best wool producers in the world both from the quality point of view of their fleece and volume per sheep.'

Jack responded 'Yes I have heard of them but you're the first owner I've spoken with who has some.' He continued. 'If you look to the left you will see another barn that we built exclusively for sheep. The old one was too small for our flock.

We still try to shear during the good weather but nowadays if we have some unexpected rain we can bring around a hundred sheep inside for a week to dry their fleece. We intend to start shearing within the month.'

John nodded and asked. 'I'd like to see the inside.' Jack and he walked to the doorway. The sheep barn had a lower ceiling than the main barn and was divided into three sections. The large holding area occupied half of the barn with the other two parts having some smaller holding pens and six bays for the shearers to do their shearing. It was different from John's shearing shed. His shearing set up had two large holding yards, both outside and at the opposite sides of the shed. They had five small gates where the sheep were exited to the shearers. After being shorn, the sheep were pushed through the opposite gate out into the other yard.

John explained his layout and commented. 'Our weather is much warmer and we have less rain so we don't need an internal holding area. But I must admit that this barn is quite practical' He turned to Jack saying 'Thanks for showing me around, I'll meet with you later. I'm off to do the social rounds.'

Meeting with other relatives and friends had taken up most of John's first week. He now decided to visit Manchester, and to take Jack with him to meet with some of the spinning mills owners. He would be embarking for his return to Victoria in three weeks' time. So, time was valuable. He and Jack left early the next morning driving a 'Two in hand' large gig. They drove for three days, changing horses twice, before reaching Manchester. He had selected three of the largest mills to visit. Each owner treated John as royalty when he introduced himself.

Yes, they all wanted super fine wool from the Merino sheep. After much discussion, John and the mill owners then arranged a direct shipping agreement, between each of them. These agreements removed both his and Michael's Liverpool and Melbourne brokers as their intermediaries. They would now only use shipping agents.

John's shipping agent in Melbourne could co-ordinate all the Kyneton district wool suppliers. It was a 'win-win' situation for all. After their last meeting with the Mills owners, Jack and he wasted no time and immediately headed back to Lazonby. They changed horses twice again, arriving home with their own horses. His father was delighted with both John's and

Michael's initiative and congratulated him heartily on his successful negotiations.

That afternoon, John heard his name called from the house, he turned to see his sister, who asked. 'Can you come up to the house? Father wishes to speak with you.'

As he walked to the house he looked out over the paddocks and compared the almost perpetual green grass of England to the Australian grass which varied from green to light brown throughout the year and yet he probably had the best sheep breed available for wool quality and volume, to supply the Manchester wool mills, and yet they grazed on poorer soil.

His father was in his study and rose to greet him when he entered. They shook hands and he sat down at the desk, facing his father. His father looked serious. He could now see that he had aged gently over the seven years. He hadn't noticed last night due to the emotion at the time. His father stood up and went to his safe and took out a rather official envelope. He sat down and opened the envelope and extracted a document. John could see that it was a Will.

His father looked at John for a second or two. He handed the Will to John saying. 'I want you to read my Will and give me your comments.' John opened the Will; it had the texture and appearance of old English parchment paper. He read the document slowly, endeavouring to absorb the intent of each sentence. It took several minutes to read. He handed it back to his father without comment, waiting for him to speak first.

His father commenced. 'John as you can see there are many legal sentences in the Will but to summarise, as you are the oldest, you therefore are the heir to Brackenshire — our main farm. Maryanne and David are being well provided. Maryanne will inherit the Brockleton farm and David the Scaleby farm.

The Will includes the contents and stock with each farm. My

shares and stocks are to be liquidated to cash. Half of the cash is to be equally divided between you three, while your mother would retain the other half and would remain at Brackenshire for the rest of her days.'

He continued. 'If your mother 'passes on' before me, her assets would be shared between the three of you, with the exception of her jewellery. The attached codicil leaves most of her jewellery to Maryanne, with a few items to each of you boys for your womenfolk. The Will also caters for the demise of either of you children before me, and how it would be shared.' He paused. 'One final point, Jack and Ann have been with us for many years and are to live out their final days here and to be cared for as if they were family.'

John sat there quietly looking at his father. He had suddenly realised that after this visit, he may not see his father again and his father had considered this distinct possibility. It was a fact of life — another seven years! The Will had needed to be shown to him during this visit. What should John say! Be honest and say the obvious.

He responded. 'Yes, I think that the Will is simple and fair and covers all aspects. Have Maryanne and David seen it yet?'

His father answered. 'Not as yet. Your return has given me the opportunity that I needed, to discuss the Will with you first. I had been considering writing to you concerning the matter but I feel more comfortable speaking with you.'

He added. 'Naturally your mother has read it and I will speak with Maryanne now and when David returns from his travels with his company in London, I'll speak with him then. I want each of you to be happy with my decision and not have any dissent when I'm no longer here.'

John said. 'I can appreciate why you are doing this but I would like to think that you will have many more comfortable years to come'.

His father nodded acknowledging John's words. They both stood up and went to join the women in the breakfast room. His father soon left him with the women, who then started to ask random questions concerning his life in the Colonies. How was his wife? What were the house and the farm like? Was he still involved in the Military? What were the Aborigines like and were they dangerous? Was it hot all the time? They already knew some of the answers but they still wanted John to answer their questions again. They chattered to and fro for over two hours when they decided to have lunch.

After lunch, Maryanne suggested that John and her drive to Lazonby. Holding John's arm, she led him to the gig that Jack had already prepared, playfully helping him step up into it. She soon had the horse clipping along at a steady and comfortable pace. The road was generally free of holes but some bumps had him holding the side rail tightly. The country side was bathed in sunlight with many of the roadside bushes and plants colourful with their flowers, creating a serene and scenic picture.

Maryanne chattered away but John was hardly listening, he was more intent picking out farms and landmarks which he could recall from his youth. After a twenty minutes' drive, Maryanne stopped the gig at the top of the hill leading down into the town of Lazonby. Below them was the small but busy hamlet that served as a hub for the local farming community. Behind the town, they could see the imposing spire of the church of St Nicholas. It had a grave yard in which many of the Hall predecessors were interred.

Moving down into the town they stopped outside the main store, demounted and tethered the horse. As they walked along the main street, John became aware that there were many more shops established since he was last here. The town had grown two-fold but still retained its country atmosphere.

They strolled along the main street. Several times they entered a shop which was owned by an old school friend and he was pleasantly surprised at the welcome he was given. After a few minutes chatting he would move on and meet more acquaintances of years gone by. He had been remembered.

Maryanne interrupted his thoughts saying. 'It's time we made our way home.' They remounted the gig and trotted out of town. John looked at his sister as she sat there holding the reins. She had said nothing of her life over the previous seven years, even in the letters she sent him.

He asked rather boldly. 'Is there a man in your life, you're an attractive woman, I had imagined that you would be married by now?'

Maryanne kept looking ahead. 'There had been a man, George Day you met him at your farewell dance.' She paused. 'He was killed in a horse stall by a stallion four years ago, I still miss him.'

She paused again and John waited, he sensed she had more to say. 'At the moment, I have a very good friend who I probably will marry, he has asked me twice and I haven't said 'no'. It took me a long time to get over George's death. His name is William McCarthy, he's a local farmer. I'll invite him to dinner for you to meet him.'

John nodded and said 'Good, I'd like that.'

The farm appeared around the corner. John asked Maryanne 'What's David's wife like? I had hoped to meet them both before I return.'

Maryanne laughed and said. 'Correction, there are now three of them, Ilsa has a two months old daughter'. John had forgotten, Maeve had told him several months ago that Ilsa was pregnant.

Maryanne continued 'You may be gone by the time David and Ilsa will be home. Father wrote to him telling him you were home, but he travels a lot from his base in London. Hopefully he will receive the letter in time.' Maryanne stopped the gig at the stable and handed the reins to Jack for him to unharness the horse.

John had settled into his family life again. Over the two last weeks he had visited their other farms and the staff with his father. They had driven to Penrith and met with the local bank manager and the family solicitor.

Then they proceeded to the office of the County Member of Parliament, the local Magistrate's office and finally to see the Mayor. His father was ensuring his heir was being introduced to those who counted in the district. That evening they dined with the members of the Agriculture Society, a group of well to do district farmers. Previously his father had been the chairman of the society and naturally was well known throughout the district.

They stayed overnight at the Penrith Hotel and returned home the following morning. John had enjoyed his father's company. They had become very close in the short time he had been home.

Breakfast was served at 8 am sharp. This was when the family planned the daily activities for the farm or visits to town for supplies or to the other farms. Jack attended breakfast with the family. This morning Jack was missing. His father looked out of the large bay window, wondering where he might be.

Suddenly Jack rushed in saying. 'Excuse me, but wild dogs have killed six of our sheep.' John took the initiative and looked at him and said 'Let's have breakfast first and then we can discuss this further.' His father nodded agreement and motioned Jack to sit with them.

The subject was not discussed during the meal; more mundane matters were the order of the day. Maryanne and her mother would drive to Lazonby to settle accounts and order a delivery of selective stock food.

John's father called Ann. 'We'll have our tea on the veranda.' John and Jack followed him out of the breakfast room.

'Well Jack, what can you tell us?' John's father asked.

Jack pointed to the top paddock and said. 'I was walking to the farmhouse when I saw the sheep running in all directions and immediately I thought of a rogue dog like the one we had one several years ago. I saddled a horse and rode towards the centre of the paddock and over near the western fence under the trees I found the sheep with their throats torn and their bodies ripped apart. I think there was more than one dog. I've sent a farm hand to collect the carcasses. I'll burn them later.'

John asked. 'Is it possible it may happen again?'

Jack nodded in the affirmative. 'Yes, we will have to shoot them or these dogs will continue to kill. This is the second incident this week. One happened at O'Brien's farm last week, he lost two ewes.'

John's father turned to Jack and said. 'Take John out and show him where you found the sheep, we may need to set traps or the like to catch or destroy these dogs.'

The two of them went to the stables, saddled their horses and rode across the paddock to the tree line. After tethering their horses to the fence, Jack led John to the blood-stained area. It was a mess of blood with bits of wool everywhere. John looked around considering his father's suggestion of setting traps. Where? It was a very large paddock. A dead sheep could be used to bait the trap, but what about the live sheep? There was no guarantee that they would not be attacked. John was standing under a tree that his brother David and he used to climb when they were youths. Jack had built them a large platform about twenty feet from the ground from there they were able to see for miles in most directions.

Jack could see him looking at the platform and said. 'Are you thinking what I'm thinking?'

John nodded. 'If we tied a dead sheep from this tree a few feet from the ground, the dogs would have to stretch to reach it. They would make good targets for a shot gun or two. Is the platform still safe to use?'

Jack replied. 'I'll send out a farm hand to check the platform and the ladder rungs as well. He can fit new ones if they're needed.'

They returned to the stables where John's father was waiting. He asked 'Can we use traps?'

John shook his head. 'No, we're considering using bait at the old tree with the platform and shooting them.'

His father said 'Good, but before you do anything, go and report this wild dog problem to the constabulary in Lazonby. I'd like you to do it today.'

John nodded, remounted his horse and cantered down the carriageway to the main road. The ride was casual, he only saw two other horsemen travelling the other way. He waved to them, while wondering what type of farmer would have wild dogs or would not realise that their dogs had gone feral? The constable was not surprised at the wild dog's report. He had had four reports in the last three weeks. One farmer had seen the dogs and said that they were brown hounds and that there were six or seven of them. The dogs had killed in an area of four square miles. Several farms had hounds but the owners said they kept their dogs locked up at night.

John told the constable that he planned to shoot the dogs if they entered his father's property. The constable shrugged shoulders and said. 'It's your right Sir. I know your father, he runs an excellent farm. I hope you destroy these vermin.'

Jack and John checked the condition of the platform. Even

though it hadn't been used for years, it was still solid and a few extra-long nails were all that was needed to tighten the base boards. They slaughtered an old ewe and suspended her four feet from the ground. This would give them a better chance to shoot the wild dogs as they jumped up to the dead ewe. That night the flock was driven to the nearest home paddock. As night darkened, John and Jack were driven to the tree platform with food and water and two shotguns with several cartridges.

It was an ideal night, no wind and with a full moon and no cloud. They could clearly see across the paddocks for several hundreds of yards. The waiting had become monotonous. It was some three hours after they had ascended the platform, that Jack touched John's shoulder and pointed to the west. In the distance, you could see the dogs. They were running low and quietly in a small pack. They suddenly stopped a few hundred yards away from the platform. John thought that they had been sensed. But no! He was wrong. The dogs ran towards them seeking the dead sheep bait. They stopped again ten yards from the bait and looked around. Then the pack attacked the carcass! Their ferocity was frightening to see. They leapt up at the bait and hung by their jaws attempting to tear the flesh away.

Jack fired two shots in quick succession and immediately two dogs fell dead. John fired just after him and killed another one. His second shot was blocked partly by one of Jack's dogs falling into his line of sight.

The shot however did hit the dog in the shoulder. It quickly sped away limping. The other dogs had run off quickly all heading in the same direction. John and Jack watched and marked the direction on the floor of the platform. John would take a compass bearing tomorrow and then visit the police station. The local constable had a survey map of the district.

They returned to the farm and both enjoyed a good night's

sleeps, comfortable with the knowledge that they would have a good chance to locate the owner of the wild dog pack tomorrow.

The constable looked rather apprehensively at John, unsure if this would help him to find the dog pack. He laid the local map on the table and stood back allowing John to rule a pencil line along the compass heading he had identified. John stood back and pointed to two farms on that compass track.

The constable nodded slowly and said slowly. 'You could be right; the Lowry's farm is a mess and he has several hounds. The other farm belongs to an old widow. She only has a small lap dog. We did check with the Lowry's but I must admit I wasn't totally satisfied that it wasn't their dogs. He has a large dog pack locked up in a barn, I checked it and it appeared to be sound.' The constable agreed to visit the Lowry farm again. John and two other owners, who had lost sheep, would go with him.

Edward Smith, one of the owners, said quietly to John. 'I have a bitch in season. I'll cage her and bring her along in my gig. If his dogs are getting out, we'll soon know.' John smiled and agreed it was a good idea.

At day break the four of them travelled in their gigs to the Lowry farm. The constable banged on the front door and was greeted with 'snide remarks' from Tom Lowry, the older son. Old Man Lowry then appeared. The constable explained the reason for the visit, saying that the wild dogs were seen heading in this direction and that he wanted to see if their hounds were all in his barn.

Old Man Lowry seemed unconcerned and said 'Let's look together, come on.' They walked to the barn where the dogs were barking furiously. It did look secure.

He turned to the group and said 'Well, are you satisfied again?'

Edward Smith said 'It looks solid. I'll head off now.'

He walked back to his gig and drove it forward along the

front of the barn. The dogs were now louder than ever. Suddenly two dogs appeared from the back of the barn and tried to climb into Edward's gig. They had smelt the bitch.

Old Man Lowry stood there stunned. 'How did they get out?'

The constable and John went to the back of the barn just in time to see another dog escaping. Behind a small scrub, a side panel was hanging vertically but it was not secured at the base. Tom Lowry and his brother Robert had been standing watching the drama. The dogs were Tom's.

Old man Lowry turned to Tom and said, 'You're a fool, these dogs are your responsibility and it's your problem.' He turned and then walked back to the farm house.

The constable looked at Tom and said 'I'll be in touch with you. In the meantime fix that barn properly to keep the dogs in and make sure that you do not leave the district.' He paused 'Gentlemen, shall we go?' The four of them left, feeling satisfied that the problem had been well and truly identified.

John was due in Liverpool for his return voyage in seven days' time and as Jack was heading into town for supplies the next day, he decided to go with him and bid farewell to some friends. On arrival, they tethered the gig outside the general store which was alongside the inn. They agreed to meet back there in an hour's time.

John visited his friends exchanging the normal pleasantries of farewells and then strolled back to the gig. Jack was leaning against it chatting to a local farmer. All of a sudden Jack stood up and looked towards the inn.

Tom Lowry and his brother Robert had walk out of the inn after a drinking bout. They had seen Jack and were approaching him and shouting at him. 'You work for the Hall's, don't you? They're nothing but trouble makers. Tell them to stay out of our way.'

John arrived behind them and said 'Tell them yourself.'

Tom turned and saw John and immediately swung a punch at him, it struck hard him on the shoulder. Tom's punching action had been so violent that he had thrown himself off balance and spun him around. His back was now towards John. John saw his chance and struck Tom hard, with a straight arm and open palm blow, in the middle of his back.

Tom staggered, tripped and then fell forward into the combination seat/table setting outside the inn. He had ended up with his body jammed between the seat and under the table top with only his legs protruding.

Robert had crept up on John and was about to hit from behind but Jack had seen him move. Jack grabbed an axe handle from the gig and in one action, knelt down on one knee and swung the handle hard at Robert's knee. The axe handle struck his knee at an angle. Robert's knee cap was immediately shattered with some knee ligaments being crushed. He collapsed to the ground screaming while clutching his injured knee.

The constable heard the commotion from his nearby gaol house and rushed to the scene while busily buttoning up his uniform jacket. 'Hello! Hello! What's all this about?' He asked — to nobody in particular.

The Innkeeper elected himself spokesman and answered the question by saying. 'The Lowrys were in a mean mood today and were looking for trouble and when they picked on Mr. Hall and Jack, they found their 'trouble.' Serves them right I say.' Several bar patrons, standing nearby, nodded in agreement.

Tom was still stuck in the table, yelling. 'Get me out.' While Robert was sitting against the inn wall clutching his injured knee and moaning in pain.

The constable quickly summed up the situation and asked John 'Do you wish to say something?'

John replied 'No. The Innkeeper is correct. They started the fight.'

The constable said 'Right, let's get Tom out of there and two of you help Robert to my cell. Innkeeper have you got some sort of a lever to lift the table panels up?'

The Innkeeper and some helpers soon had Tom free. The constable then marched him to the cell to join his brother.

On the way home John looked at Jack curiously and asked 'Who taught you that axe handle trick?' Jack laughed and said 'There's an Asian print in your hallway at the farm house showing a Chinese warrior performing the same action. It works well, doesn't it?' John smiled and nodded in agreement

John was now prepared to return to Victoria. His luggage had been packed and his friends had been bidden farewell. He was dreading saying farewell to his mother and father. His father was still active but his mother was showing her age and had become frail. When he departed his family and the staff were present. Obviously, David had not received his father's letter and had not returned.

John said goodbye almost by reverse seniority. First, he shook hands with the general staff, then Anne, and Jack followed by his sister and brother, his mother and finally his father. His mother, Maryanne and Anne were in tears. His father looked sad but he had accepted the fact that John must return to Victoria. It was where his future lay. He was well established there and more importantly he was married with a family. He shook hands with his father, hugged him, then abruptly turned and climbed into the gig with Jack. He waved until he and Jack reached the end of the driveway and the gig turned towards Penrith. He then wiped his eyes.

On arrival at the Penrith Coach house, Jack wished John well and assured him that he would keep his eye on his family and that he would write to him from time to time. Jack placed John's baggage on the Stagecoach, they shook hands. A quick wave and they went their separate ways. They would always be friends, even from afar.

The trip to Liverpool was uneventful. He was a day early but the ship was ready and he was welcomed aboard by the First Officer. He was the first passenger to arrive.

He was glad of the solitude when he was shown to his cabin. He lay on the bunk for a few hours while thinking of nothing and everything. When his head was clear he decided to take a walk on deck. Perhaps Captain Badger was on board? The ship had a slow rocking motion and John found it calming.

He was leaning on guard rail looking at the small rowing boats on the water plying their trade, when he became aware of a person standing by him. Turning he looked into the smiling face of Captain Badger. 'Welcome aboard Mr. Hall. How was your visit? Successful I hope.'

'Hello Captain. Yes, it was a most successful and a very pleasant visit.'

At this time, back home in Kyneton, a very sad event had occurred. Maeve walked into the kitchen made a cup of tea and sat down looking out the window when she asked the boys. 'Where is your grandfather?'

He was always up and dressed early. The boys looked at her but said nothing. Maeve went to the stable and asked Connor?

He replied 'I'll ride out and have a look for him. I harnessed a gig for him to take out this morning.' Connor soon returned, driving the gig Edmund had taken out earlier, with his horse tied behind the gig. He jumped down and said 'He's had an accident, He's fallen from the gig and I think he is dead.'

Maeve went to her father who was lying on the gig seat, not moving. Connor and the boys moved his body into his bedroom.

Connor had then remounted his horse and gone for the Doctor. Maeve broke into tears. The maid helped her to her bed and sat with her for company while attempting to console her.

When the Doctor arrived, he made an examination of Edmund's body and then confirmed that he had died from a broken neck. Connor said he believed that he had fallen backwards from the gig and contacted the ground first with the back of his head.

The Doctor stated 'That would explain the sign of the impact injury to his neck' The Doctor wrote out the death certificate and handed it to Connor. Maeve was still indisposed. The doctor said he would arrange for the mortician to remove Edmund's body and that he would notify the Coroner's Office. Connor then rode over to 'Woodlea' farm to tell Michael the bad news.

Michael sat quietly for while on the veranda, Mary brought a cup of tea and left him to his thoughts. She felt for him but she knew not to intrude in his grieving. The next day Mary and he drove to 'Sunnyside' farm to offer comfort to Maeve. Michael put on a brave face but inwardly he was upset. Maeve was now composed but when Michael hugged her, she cried again. Naturally the boys and Mary, even Connor was upset at the unexpected death of a very dear relative and a close friend.

The Coroner's Inquest was straight forward. It was not unusual for Edmund to ask Connor to harness a gig for him to take a drive around the property. That particular day Edmund had driven out onto the main road where Edmund's body was found alongside a large wheel rut hole full of water. Connor had found that the left side wheel was wet and muddy and it appeared that his gig wheel had entered the rut and tipped sufficiently sideways to throw Edmund out of the seat.

After he had been thrown from the gig he had fallen backwards and landed with his head striking the ground first.

Edmund must not have been aware of the rut so it was possible that because of his age, he had been inattentive. It was ruled that death occurred by 'Misadventure'.

With Edmund being a member of the well-known Hall family it was only natural that the funeral would be attended by many of the town and farming community. The hearse was a magnificent black enamelled four-wheel vehicle with side glass panels enclosing the coffin and the wreaths. It was towed by two all black horses with their black leather harness highly polished. Each horse had a feathered attachment on the top of their head gear which completed the impressive scene. A lone piper led the entourage from the church to the cemetery. They all walked slowly and silently, each with their own thoughts. Fortunately, the weather was overcast and cool. The graveside service did not take long and the entourage then headed back to the Mechanics Institute for the wake.

All the town leaders of commerce and business and of course the politicians and councillors were in attendance. As is said in many farming communities, most only meet at births, weddings and funerals. The wake was held in the Kyneton Mechanics Institute with many of those attending, personally offering their condolences.

Maeve and the boys only stayed for a short time, with Michael's family leaving shortly after them. It had been a demanding day for the two families. Maeve felt it more than the others being without John's support, who was still on the high seas.

Captain Badger and John had become friends and he was frequently invited to dine at the Captain's table. There were twenty passengers in the main deck cabins and twenty in steerage below the quarter deck. The steerage passengers were a motley group, five of them were from the South African mines and were inclined to be boisterous but they gave no indication of the trouble to come. Initially, the voyage itself was without incident. The seas being reasonably calm with good winds and some sunny days, with their first land fall due to be Cape Town. The ship had ample water and food for three months sailing. Its cargo was mainly general goods such as furniture, bedding, cooking utensils and some machinery destined for a new Victorian spinning mill for their blankets production.

Trouble started without warning, when the ship turned to enter Cape Town harbour. Two of the miners had gone to the Captain's cabin and broken open his gun cabinet and stolen his two pistols.

The ring leader then climbed the steps to the quarter deck with his mate following him, and levelled his pistol at Captain Badger and said that he and the other miners were taking over the ship. He then ordered the Captain to change course and sail to Durban. The helmsman looked at the Captain, who nodded to him to change course.

Meanwhile the other three, who were armed with knives had locked the steerage passengers in the aft hold and had then locked the off-duty crew in their quarters. The six crewmen, who were on deck duty, had had their knives removed under gun point by the other armed mutineer. The crewmen were silent but very angry.

The miners, albeit mutineers, told the male main deck passengers that they were to help the duty crew and would only be allowed on deck after their cabins had been searched for guns or knives. John had bought his revolver with him but had kept it hidden it in the false bottom of his sea chest.

The ship sailed from the harbour and headed out to sea again. After a small lunch was served, the mutineers relaxed a little assuming they had everything under control. John had wandered back to his cabin and retrieved his revolver and put it in his belt under his coat tails. He wandered up to the quarter deck steps and looking around he could see that only two of the mutineers had pistols.

The leader of the mutineers saw John standing there and ordered him to. 'Get me some more food.' John nodded and went to galley and returned with a piece of beef and a small loaf of bread. He climbed up the steps and handed the food to the leader, who after putting his pistol in his belt. He took the bread in one hand and the beef in the other.

When the leader turned away to eat, John pulled out his revolver and levelled it at the other mutineer, who had his pistol in his hand and ordered 'Drop your pistol!'

When the mutineer turned to look at John he began to lift his pistol. John fired and shot him in the shoulder. The impact of the bullet caused him to spin around. He stumbled off balance to the guard rail, missed grabbing it and fell over the side into the sea and vanished. John quickly put his pistol to the neck of the shocked ring leader who immediately raised his hands into the air, dropping his food. John then removed the pistol from his belt.

The drowned mutineer's pistol had fallen onto the ship's deck and was quickly picked up by Captain Badger. When the shot was heard, all eyes turned to the quarter deck. Captain Badger, with the pistol in his hand, could be seen to be in charge again. The duty crew turned to face the three other mutineers who had pulled their knives. Captain Badger commanded, with his pistol pointing at them. 'Drop your knives or be shot. You have three seconds, — one — two!'

Three knives immediately dropped to the deck and were quickly collected by some of the duty crew. The crew then gave the three mutineers a beating until they were told to stop by the Captain.

The ship was soon returned to normal and then sailed back

into Cape Town harbour. The passengers and crew were all happy that the drama was over but secretly they were thrilled to be involved in such excitement. They would all have a story to tell to all and sundry for years to come.

The leader of the mutineers later admitted they were involved with a smuggling gang attempting to hijack a diamond shipment from Durban. The four mutineers were handed over to the South African Authorities. None of the men were known to them. They were not South African nationals but they could expect no leniency by the law. Penalties were severe for crimes committed on the high seas, regardless of a pirates' nationality.

Several days later at dinner one evening, while crossing the Indian Ocean, John asked the Captain Badger 'Would you have shot the mutineers?'

The Captain thought for a moment and then replied. 'Yes and no. Initially 'yes', I was so angry but 'no' when I was back in command.'

John smiled and said 'As a former military officer, I know what you mean. It's the difference between being or not being in control of your domain.'

The remainder of the trip was slow and uneventful and they were soon navigating the notorious entrance to Port Phillip Bay known as 'The Heads' and sailing up the Bay to eventually anchor in Hobson's Bay near Melbourne. John stayed in Melbourne for the night and early next morning boarded the coach for Kyneton and home.

His joy at being home again with his family was mixed with sadness, when he was told of Edmund's passing. Michael and Mary joined them for Sunday lunch that weekend, where John again went through a series of questions and answers from both of the families about his visit. He enjoyed the banter within the family and was pleased that the farm and business had continued successfully in his absence. Particularly Maeve's handling of the water rights issue.

CHAPTER FOUR

Homeward Bound

Michael and Tabu stopped and looked back at the town of Echuca. From the hill they were on, the town looked smaller than before. It was picturesque with the morning sun casting long shadows from the gum trees along the Murray river bank. The river was flowing fast and several large trees could be seen floating downstream. They would cause the riverboat Captains some concern for the security of the hull of their boats. Their broken branches could put a serious hole in a wooden boat hull very easily. Michael mused perhaps Echuca would be an important inland port and farming centre in years to come. He was pleased that he had accomplished his exploration of the country to the east of Echuca. Even though they had been away from home for nearly three months, he felt that the time had been well spent.

He turned to Tabu and said 'Let's go home'. He gave his horse a spur and headed south for home. Tabu was driving the four-wheel wagon with one horse in harness and the spare horses tied to the tail gate. The two dogs were up in the wagon and would sleep most of the time. The wagon had endured the trip without any major failure although a wheel spoke had sheared and required changing at a blacksmith's, before leaving Echuca. Michael and Tabu had to sit at the 'Smithy's' for half a day watching and waiting for the spoke to be replaced. The spoke hole in the wooden wheel rim had split and had allowed the spoke to move back and forth and to eventually shear at the insert. The blacksmith and his brother complimented each other with their skills. The brother was a cooper and was the maker of excellent barrels for the local brewery.

After the blacksmith had removed the steel rim, the cooper manufactured a new spoke and a new section to be inserted into the wooden rim. After they were fitted to form the wheel, the blacksmith then expanded the steel rim by heating it in his forge. He then placed the steel rim around the wooden wheel and quenched it with copious quantities of water to shrink the steel rim tightly onto the wooden wheel. Steam and smoke billowed everywhere. The repaired wheel would outlast the life of the wagon.

They continued south towards Rochester, over the same route they had used coming north, at a slow but steady rate. They were in no hurry, not wanting to work the horses too hard. The horses were still in good condition after the long journey and continued to plod along steadily. The distance to the town was around sixteen miles and would take them less than two days. The grasslands had become boring and Michael found himself thinking of Mary and home. Occasionally a mob of kangaroos would hop by or emus would come up to them, stare at them for a few minutes and then speed away into the distance.

On one occasion, the dogs spotted an old man kangaroo close to them and gave chase. Michael raced after the dogs calling them to — stop! But they ignored him and were too quick for his horse to catch up to them.

The kangaroo headed for a lagoon, stood in shallow water and turned ready to fight. The dogs followed him into the water. His claws scored several cuts on the dogs as they circled him but then he backed into deeper water, lost his footing and drowned. The last they saw of him as he sank below the water was his tail pointing skywards. Michael had been concerned for his dogs, as kangaroos had been known to drown dogs by holding them underwater with their front paws. This time the dogs had survived with only a few cuts. He washed the dogs' cuts with salt and water and then put some axle grease on them to keep the flies off the wounds.

Tabu was looking at smoke in the distance, unsure if it was a camp fire or a shrub fire, but he could see no aborigines. They were watchful in case the smoke was from a bush fire, as it could become close and dangerous very quickly. The wind direction was all important and they needed to keep an eye on it. Generally, the wind was from the west or the north and this fire was to the east of them. They were not too concerned.

The weather was dry and sunny with a light breeze. They slept under the wagon each night enjoying the clear starry sky. Michael had allowed three days to reach Rochester, three days to Elmore, seven days to Heathcote and another seven to Kyneton. Barring any mishaps, he would be home in about three weeks.

He had written to Mary telling her he would be home within a month, so an early arrival would be a pleasant surprise. The country town mail service was improving and he expected that the letter would reach home within a week. He missed her idle chatter and watching her pottering around the garden. The flowers and vegetable garden would be all a mass of colour this month. Her small orchard always had some fruit ready to pick. It would be good to be home again.

They arrived at Rochester in early evening and set up camp on the outskirts of the town. Tabu did not like going into any town, he had suffered plenty of verbal abuse because of his race. Even Michael could not protect him from this problem.

Michael went to the general store first thing the following morning to collect some supplies. They were low on food for the horses and the dogs needed some fresh meat.

As he tied up the wagon, a voice hailed him. 'Are you Michael Somerset?'

Michael turned, looked at the fellow and answered. 'Yes, that's me, what can I do for you?'

The fellow was the local grocer. He replied 'Bert Mustey of Riverview Station asked me to look out for you. He wants you to take some sheep to Heathcote.'

Michael thought, why not. We're going that way. 'Where is the station?'

The grocer replied 'It's on your way south, turn left about five miles out of town. You will see the sign. Follow it and you will be at the farm house within an hour. You won't get lost.'

After he purchased his supplies, Michael headed back to camp and told Tabu that they would have a short droving job during the trip south. They were both pleased to have something to do, as the trip had become monotonous.

The sign post and mail box were old and dilapidated but the sign was still readable. 'Riverview Station — three miles'. The road to the station was in poor condition. The rain had washed away the light soil and had left rocks and small pebbles as a road surface. Michael let the horses find their own way up the road. He didn't want injuries to their hoofs or any loosening of horseshoes. They eventually arrived at a large wooden gate with a crossbar over the top signed 'Riverview'. A track was leading up to the farm house.

The farm house was perched on the top of a hill, with the left side of the road following a river course. It was a serene setting, the slow flowing river, sheep grazing in green paddocks and a farm house surrounded by colourful flowers. The farmer had made an excellent choice on where to settle. Two barking dogs came running down to meet them, a man had appeared on the farmhouse porch and waved to them.

After the normal introductions, Bert Mustey invited him into the farm house and introduced him to Bridget, his Irish wife.

Over a cup of tea and scones they started chatting. He was a self-made man, both he and his wife had been pioneers to the district. They had driven a covered wagon from Melbourne over ten years ago and had lived in a tent for three years.

During that time they had worked seven days a week building the farm house, the sheds and fences. They felled the trees and cut all their planks and poles with a dual handled cross cut saw. Initially river clay had been used for floors and sealing gaps in the walls. They had cleared a paddock to grow corn and maize and purchased two cows. Five years ago he bought some Merino sheep from a drover travelling from New South Wales. Bert had not worried whether the drover owned the sheep or not, he bought a ram and forty ewes from him. Since then he had swapped his ram each year and had now bred a fine flock of Merinos.

Bert had known Hedley Rooke for several years, the New South Wales station owner to whom Michael had delivered his sheep last month. He had sold him sheep in the past. They had met in Echuca recently where Hedley had mentioned to Bert that Michael would be returning via Rochester within the next few weeks. Bert had then asked the Rochester grocer to keep an eye out for Michael — the drover with the aborigine. Most travellers visited the local grocer, hence the grocer being Bert's message man.

Michael was still unsure of why Bert wished to see him. After discussing his farm, Bert suddenly said 'I have sold forty ewes and eight young rams to a Mr. Francis, a broker in Heathcote. He has buyers for each of the rams and for the flock of forty ewes. I would like you to deliver them for me. I will give you two young rams in payment. They have only just been weaned, so they will still be looking for their mothers for milk. Their mothers are in the flock. Well, what do you think, can you deliver them for me?'

'Can I see the sheep first?' asked Michael.

Bert stood up and said 'Certainly, follow me.' The sheep were penned close by and a quick look verified that they were first class sheep and that the rams were healthy.

It was a reasonable payment, a good ram was always in demand in order to maintain a first class flock. He would keep one ram and give the other to John. Michael nodded and said. 'Yes. I can put the young rams in the wagon most of the time to wean them from their mothers.'

Bert said. 'I will place a letter in our mail box to be collected by Cobb & Co and delivered to Mr. Francis, advising him to be watching out for you in about a week or two weeks' time. He lives in Heathcote opposite the Commercial Hotel.'

Droving the sheep would delay his return by a few days but with luck he would still arrive home within a day or so from when he would be expected.

Michael nodded agreement and said. 'We will camp here tonight and leave at daybreak.'

They shook hands in agreement, Bert replied. 'Good, now please join us for dinner.'

Michael enjoyed the evening, both the meal and the idle chatter of an isolated woman and her husband. He felt lonely, being without Mary, in this atmosphere. Tabu as usual had vanished nearby. He would be at the wagon in the morning.

At day break, Tabu and he fed the animals and after a satisfactory inspection of the horses' hooves, hitched one horse to the wagon and tied the others to the tailgate, they loaded ten noisy rams. They would continue to bleat for the first hour before settling down.

Michael waved farewell. Bert's wife continued to wave until they were almost out of sight. It would be a lonely life out here for a woman. Any company, however fleeting, would be welcome.

The small flock was easy to control. Michael soon identified the leader of the flock and he kept his eye on her. The dogs were running again and seemed happier tailing the sheep rather than sitting in the wagon doing nothing.

Tabu was driving the wagon leading the sheep, most of the time he was half asleep. The horse just had to follow the road. The road surface was reasonable, although every now and then, where a rut had been formed by rainwater and passing bullock teams, it was necessary to leave the road. Michael rode behind the flock ensuring the sheep didn't stray.

They saw very few other travellers during their time on the road. Two of the horseman they did see, kept wide of them, Michael waved to them but the response was rather vague. He was to find out later that they were more interested in his sheep, than Michael realised. Generally, riders stopped and exchanged the news of the day, bushranger activity, the weather, country accidents and so on, but not these two riders. Michael dismissed them from his mind and thought of home and Mary.

The next town they would arrive at was Elmore, some twelve miles south. You always knew when you were heading south, the sun would be at your right and at noon it would be level with shoulders.

The country was mainly flat grass lands. They would encounter few hills until they reached the outskirts of Heathcote. This was at edge of the mountain range that separated the inland plains from the coastal plains. From Heathcote to Kyneton he would have several long climbs and descents.

They arrived at Elmore at noon. Tabu took over the flock of sheep and avoided the town, while Michael took the wagon with the rams into town. He unloaded the rams into a council holding paddock and fed them. Some were still not happy with solid food, but they were learning.

He then drove the wagon to the main street and after tying

up the horses, he went for a walk past the shops. It was the first time that he had stopped here. It was a small town but the shops were well stocked and adequately catered for the farmers.

He stopped at an inn to have an ale and lunch and was pleased to see some Kyneton farmers who he knew. He stayed a while telling them of his exploits over the last few months and his current job droving some sheep for Bert Mustey. They replied by saying that the Kyneton train service had started. It had already attracted more visitors and the town looked like it would become a major farming centre. Michael was delighted with the news, enjoying the meeting but he needed to move on. He gave his apologies and headed back to the council pen.

When he reached the pen, he was surprised to see several people around the enclosure. He nodded and walked past them and entered the pen to feed the rams.

A voice behind him asked. 'What are you doing with my sheep?'

Michael turned and saw a long haired lean man looking at him. Michael was astounded. He said. 'I beg your pardon, but these rams are mine!'

The long-haired man replied 'We'll see about that, I'm calling the Constable.'

Michael said. 'Do what you like.' He sat down near the wagon, shaking his head in amazement.

When the Constable arrived, he questioned Michael first and asked. 'Are these your sheep? Sir.'

Michael replied 'Yes.'

The Constable asked. 'Have you documents to that effect?'

Michael then realised that he had been given no documents. He answered 'No, I am delivering these for Bert Mustey to Francis the Broker in Heathcote.'

The Constable then asked the long hair man. 'Mr. Parrot. Are these your sheep and do you have documents to prove it?'

Mr Parrot alias the long-haired man replied. 'Look they have my brand on them.'

Michael looked in the pen and realised that there were more than ten rams in the pen and that some were branded.

The Constable looked at Michael and said 'Well Sir, you have some explaining to do.'

Neither Bert nor he had anticipated this situation occurring. The Constable and Mr. Parrot were talking quietly in the corner.

The Constable came back looking grave and said. 'I believe that these sheep belong to Mr. Parrott, however Mr. Parrott does not wish to press charges, so be on your way now.'

Michael was unsure how far he could argue with the Constable and did not immediately answer.

A voice said 'What's going on here Constable?' It was the local Sergeant.

The Constable related the events and his decision. The Sergeant looked at Mr. Parrot and asked. 'What have you been up to now Parrot?'

Mr. Parrot said nothing. The Sergeant walked to the pen and counted, he turned and said. There are six branded rams and ten unbranded.

The Sergeant asked Parrot. 'Why aren't the merino rams branded you have only branded the crossbreds.'

Parrot replied 'I've been very busy and I missed them.'

The Sergeant turned to Michael and asked 'Why didn't Mr. Mustey brand them.'

Michael was unable to give him an answer.

The Sergeant was a farmer and he could see that the rams were young.

He asked Michael. 'How long is it since they have been weaned?'

'I'm weaning them now,' he replied.

'It's a pity you don't have their mothers with you, we could solve this matter in minutes.'

Michael said 'But I have, they're in a flock I have out of town.'

The Sergeant looked at Michael and said. 'You have a lot to learn son, don't travel without the paper work in future and only drove branded sheep. You Mr. Parrot are now in the care of the Constable until I say otherwise.'

The Sergeant looked at Michael and said 'Load up the rams and let's find your sheep.'

A considerable crowd had now gathered and Mr. Parrot was now looking a little uncomfortable.

Michael was unsure where Tabu had taken the sheep. His Kyneton friends had joined the crowd. Michael asked them to help find Tabu and the flock. He knew they would be within a few miles of town and just south of Elmore. The Sergeant rode along on Michael's wagon, with the rams in the back. Michael was most apprehensive, he could see that the Sergeant was not a man to upset.

An hour later Tabu was located. The wagon was driven into the centre of the flock and the unbranded young rams unloaded. Within a few minutes of searching, each ram had found its mother. The wisdom of the old Sergeant had won through.

The Constable had collected Parrot's belongings and taken them to the Police stable. He had kept Parrot away from the crowd, most of who were now following Michael's wagon.

When Michael later described Parrot to Tabu. He told Michael that he was one of the two men they had seen a few days ago and had kept their distance from them.

The Constable took Parrot to the Police stable and sat him down, instructing him not to leave. Stupidly Parrot left the stable to go to collect his horse.

He was spotted and he ran back towards stable, right into the arms of the Kyneton farmers. They marched him down past the shops to the front of the pub and tied him to the veranda post.

Someone shouted 'Let's teach him a lesson.'

An old shearer stepped forward and put Parrot in a head-lock and with shears, cut Parrot's hair as close as possible to his scalp.

A voice from the crowd called 'Tar and feather him.'

Unfortunately for Parrot, a Blacksmith's cart was next to the pub and had a cask of axle grease in the tray. With no tar readily available, the mob used the axle grease. Plucked feathers were donated by the butcher who supplied the local poultry. The feathers were liberally thrown onto the grease. Worse was to come, Parrott's trousers were pulled half way down and two emu feathers were placed between his buttocks.

Parrot was left tied up until the Sergeant stepped in. He ordered the Constable to take him to the Police stables so that he could clean himself up. The Constable was concerned that he would be seen to be collaborating with Parrot so he took the easy way out and left the stable door open for Mr. Parrot to escape into the distance. It is believed he headed west never to be seen in Victoria again.

When the Sergeant found out that the Constable had let Parrott escape, he told him that he had finally showed some initiative and helped cut down the paperwork that would have occurred if a trial had eventuated. The Sergeant believed that Mr. Parrot had been punished enough due to the extreme embarrassment he had endured and would not return to the district again. His branded rams were auctioned and the money given to the local school. That was the end of the matter, although the story was often told over an ale in the pub

Michael was to learn later that Mr. Parrot had caused trouble several times before and he had seen Michael as an easy target transporting young unbranded rams. Michael had learnt a valuable lesson.

They left the Elmore district with a feeling of relief. Michael could well have done without the drama they had encountered. They ambled out of town heading further south, they had thirty miles to go to reach Heathcote. The sheep and the other animals were all in good condition. The grasslands provided adequate food and waterholes were within a day's travel. They were averaging nearly seven miles a day, regardless of the terrain. He should reach Heathcote within a week without hurrying. Michael was satisfied with their progress, even if they had lost almost a day. A dense row of trees appeared in the distance. Michael guessed that they would be along the Campaspe River.

The closer they became to the trees, more and more birds became airborne. The sky was a mass of white cockatoos, wheeling and screeching loudly. Then a large flock of grey and pink Galahs flew high into the air and then dived earthwards. It was a spectacular sight; one which city people would never have the pleasure of seeing.

Michael leaned back in the saddle and sat watching in delight at the hundreds of birds in flight. At one stage the cockatoos settled on an open section of land and created a blanket of white while ripping onion weed out of the ground. Michael knew why he loved this country.

The road led straight to the river. The water was high and flowing quickly and was too deep for the sheep to cross. Michael sent Tabu to follow a track west along the river bank to see if he could find a shallow section of the river from where they could move the sheep across. Tabu returned after several hours to report that he had found a place where the river was much wider with shallow water flowing very slowly. Michael moved the sheep back to the grass lands and headed west adjacent the trees. They reached the crossing at sundown and decided to camp there for the night and move the sheep across in the morning.

They were awakened by the sounds of a Laughing Jackass, then another started laughing and another, until the river bank was a crescendo of noise. Although their laughing was loud, it was not unpleasant to the ear.

The river water was slow and flat. Tabu rode his horse across the area they would ford. It was three feet deep in the middle and would pose a threat to the sheep. They would not be able to feel the bottom of the river. Michael decided to use the wagon as a ferry. They emptied the wagon and removed the wheels. They then pulled the canvas sheet tightly under the wagon body up over the corners and then tied the four corner ropes together in the middle of the wagon.

Tabu rode his horse across towing a long rope. When he reached the other bank, he tied the rope around a solid tree trunk and then rode back and tied the rope to the wagon. They could not afford to lose the wagon.

After tying their legs together, they loaded eight sheep at a time into the make shift boat and then it was hauled across the river by Tabu's horse. This was repeated several times until most of the sheep were safely on the other side of the river.

The young rams were ferried in a middle load to ensure they stayed with the adult sheep on either side of the river. By themselves they may have strayed. The ferrying took all morning and had been hard work. Only one ewe had been lost. She had panicked and hurled herself out of the makeshift boat and vanished under the water.

The Aborigines in this area were of concern. Although they were distant neighbours of Tabu's tribe, they were well known for their warlike attitude.

Tabu told Michael that they had to be careful and that they

would need to remain alert both day and night. Michael knew that the dogs would give them a warning most times but they still needed to watch for an ambush. They might kill the dogs first.

He decided to travel over the grass lands. He now carried a pistol in his hip holster and a shotgun in his saddle holster. Tabu was driving the wagon and had some spears and a club alongside him on the seat.

Smoke was drifting in the sky from the direction they were travelling. It was only a small column but nevertheless it indicated aborigines could be in the area.

Michael saw no sense in attempting to avoid them now. They would know that they were in the area. They continued on with Tabu standing up on the wagon looking ahead. Then he pointed. There were three warriors two hundred yards away directly in their path. Michael could not see any spears.

Suddenly Tabu said 'Spears long foot.' The warriors did not move and Michael and Tabu continued towards them. One of the warriors yelled loudly and lifted his foot up, bringing his spear to his hand. He then waved his spear in the air. Tabu stood up and yelled back. The warrior lowered his spear and walked towards them with the other two following close to him. They now had their spears in their hands. They held the spears low but ready to throw.

Michael halted his horse. The wagon horse stopped with Tabu standing up, proud and tall. Michael sat calmly on his horse but his hand was on the butt of his pistol. The leader ignored Michael and only looked at Tabu. Neither spoke for several moments, then the warrior leader walked closer to Tabu and then he said something that made Tabu relax. Tabu climbed down from the wagon and sat down. The warriors walked up to him, sat down opposite him and started talking in a common dialect.

Tabu shoulders rounded and he had lowered his head. Michael wondered, if they knew each other, perhaps this was not good news. At least the warriors were now calm and no longer aggressive. He began to relax a little.

Tabu eventually turned to Michael and said. 'I know dem, they know tribe long me. Fader long me is Mandu he Elder, he sick. I leave Heathcote, go long fader.'

Michael nodded and said 'Yes, of course, I understand.'

Tabu and the other aborigines remained sitting on the ground and talked at length. Tabu finally stood up, that signalled the end of the meeting.

Michael gave the aborigines flour, tobacco with some sugar and salt. He would buy more in Heathcote. With a farewell wave, the aborigines departed and he and Tabu continued their way south. With the delay at the river and now with the aborigine interlude they had lost almost a full day. Michael thought, so what, at least we did not get into a confrontation.

Michael was pleased Tabu had not deserted him immediately, but he wished he could have said to him 'go now', but he was needed because of the ewes.

Tabu sat in the wagon quietly with his own thoughts. Although he and Michael related well with each other, they were from different worlds and it would remain that way. Their cultures were very different.

The grasslands were no more. They were now surrounded by trees growing in shale ground. The ground was covered in small brown sharp shale rocks.

There was little shrubbery and the trees were thin grey gums with stringy bark hanging from them, with only a vague track apparent. Rain had carved trenches across the track and made the going difficult for the wagon. Tabu took his time negotiating the best track for it, they didn't want a broken wheel so close to Heathcote, particularly with the rams on board. Even the sheep were having trouble walking on the shale.

They met several men mining for gold in the area. The men were polite but said little. Michael looked down one of the pits that they had dug. It would be hard work digging through shale and then having to find water to wash that soil in a cradle to separate the gold — if any.

That night they stopped at a creek which had some grass and enjoyed a good night's rest. The following morning they checked the hooves of the horses and sheep before moving on. One sheep had a cut in the inside of its hoof. This ewe joined the rams in the wagon.

The dogs fared surprising well seeing that they have soft pads on their paws. The horses' shoes were showing wear and would need to be replaced in Heathcote. The track had slowly improved, winding through trees with small areas of grasslands. Every now and then Tabu would dodge a low tree branch. On horseback it took some concentration as the horse would walk under trees with thin low branches forcing Michael to push the branch away or try to bend under it. Some branches required him to stop and turn the horse. He misjudged some branches and ended up with a few facial bruises and scratches. He didn't mind, they would soon be in Heathcote, where he would hand over the sheep and rams to Mr. Francis and then head for Kyneton and home.

They arrived in Heathcote in the early afternoon. Opposite the Commercial Hotel Michael saw a building with the sign — Francis Brokers. Mr. Francis was in attendance in his office and after exchanging pleasantries and paperwork, thirty-nine ewes and eight rams were driven to a paddock behind his office. The task was now complete. Michael took the horses to the local farrier to have each of them reshod. Michael and Tabu then went to the general store to stock up for their journey to Kyneton. After tying up the wagon horse Michael went inside to collect their goods. He then walked to the produce store to order some chaff. The horses had been eating grass for weeks and Michael decided that they need a change of food.

Tabu had stayed outside the general store, near the wagon leaning on veranda post. A rider rode up quickly, dismounted and then asked Tabu to hold the reins of his horse. Tabu took the reins obediently. The rider then entered the general store. Within minutes the rider ran out and snatched the reins from Tabu, mounted the horse and galloped away disappearing in a cloud of dust. Tabu just stood there looking after the rider. The storekeeper had run from the store and had seen the rider snatch the reins from Tabu.

The storekeeper started shouting 'Robbery, robbery' and grabbed Tabu by the arm repeatedly saying 'You helped him'. Tabu stood still unsure what was happening.

The constable soon arrived. The storekeeper told of the rider entering the store and pointing a pistol at him demanding money. After receiving the money, the rider ran out and mounted his horse and fled. The storekeeper insisted that Tabu had assisted the robber by holding his horse's reins.

The constable immediately arrested Tabu, although he was unsure if he had been involved in the robbery or if he had been an innocent bystander. Michael heard the commotion and wander back to the general store. To his amazement, he was told that an aborigine had been involved in a daylight robbery and had been arrested. Surely it could not be Tabu? But where was he?

Michael strode quickly to the Police station and found that it was Tabu who had been locked up. He explained to the constable that they had just arrived in Heathcote that very morning from Rochester. The constable said he had to accept the written statement of a local businessman over that of a non-local man and an aborigine. The local Justice of the Peace would hear his case tomorrow and he could decide on the evidence presented.

The constable allowed Michael to visit Tabu. He told Michael what had happened and it was apparent that he had indeed been an innocent bystander. Michael had a sleepless night as he tried to sleep under the wagon.

The court convened at 10 AM. There were several cases before Tabu's. It was a nervous wait for the two of them.

The clerk called. 'Tabu'. The constable indicated to Tabu to stand up.

The clerk said 'You are charged with aiding and abetting a robbery. How do you plea.' Tabu did not respond.

The presiding Justice of the Peace had not looked at the prisoner up to this stage. When he heard the name 'Tabu', he looked at the prisoner and immediately recognised. Tabu also recognized Mr. Frederick Wyland.

'Well, Tabu we meet again.'

He turned to the constable and asked 'What exactly did he do?'

The constable replied 'He held the reins of the robber's horse.'

'And then waited to be arrested?' queried the Justice. 'Did he have any money on him when you arrested him?'

'No.' Answered the constable.

'What did the alleged offender have to say to the Charge?' The Justice continued.

'Nothing, he hasn't spoken.' The constable said.

'Do you know anything about this man?' the Justice asked.

The constable said 'Yes. A drover came into the police station and said he worked for him and that they had arrived from Rochester yesterday morning delivering sheep to Mr. Francis the Broker.'

'Tabu, what did you do?' asked the Justice.

Tabu looked at him and said slowly. 'I hold whiteman's horse, he askim, tasal. No rob no one.'

'Call the storekeeper to the stand.' The Justice instructed, he then continued. 'What makes you think that the alleged offender aided the robbery. There is no evidence at this stage.'

'He held the reins of the robber's horse.' The storekeeper answered.

The Justice queried. 'But for what gain? We will adjourn the court for one hour'

It was noon. 'All rise' said the clerk.

Michael decided that lunch was in order and went to the Commercial hotel. Coincidently, the Justice of the Peace and the constable also came into dine in the same room. Michael saw the constable look his way and then speak to the Justice. The Justice stood up and walked towards Michael's table, he had a slight limp.

'Frederick Wyland Sir, may I join?'

Michael stood up and shook his hand and motioned him to be seated. 'Michael Somerset from Kyneton.'

Fred started. 'I knew Tabu prior to today, he saved my life a year ago. He worked for me at a gold mine I own. I am indebted to him.'

Michael said 'Yes, I value him as a friend, a farm hand and stockman. The charge is wrong! He was minding our wagon which was outside the general store, when the robbery happened.'

Michael continued 'We are on our way south. I have a property at Kyneton and Tabu is on his way back to his tribal home. His father is a tribal elder and he is dying. He has no reason to be involved in a robbery, if he needed money he would get it from me.'

The constable was waving to the Justice, it was time to go. They both stood up and shook hands.

Michael said 'Perhaps we will meet again.' Fred nodded and walk towards the constable.

The clerk called the court to order for the Justice to read out his decision.

It was predictable. Tabu stood silently showing no emotion. He did not understand why he was here.

The Justice read 'After viewing the facts presented, I find that there is no case to answer. It would appear that Tabu was an innocent bystander who thought he was doing someone a favour. The charge is dismissed.'

The Justice lent over and said a few words to the constable. The constable motioned Tabu to come with him. Michael followed them out of the courtroom and then around the back through the tack room. The constable saw Michael and invited him to join them. They entered a small room, there waiting for them was Frederick Wyland J.P. albeit — Fred. He immediately shook Tabu's hand. They all sat down.

'It's good to see you again. I have often wondered where you went after you took me to the Kilmore Doctor. I'm sorry I didn't have the opportunity to thank you for saving my life. Where did you go?' Fred asked.

'I go long Walkabout many muns. Then boss Michael gimme job wok long sheep.'

Fred laughed. 'Tabu's few words covers over a year's time.'

He continued. 'The gold mine that my late friend Tom and I found made me a wealthy man and I settled on a property just out of Heathcote. To cut a long story short, I had time on my hands and as I had had some legal training in my early days and after some further training, I ended up being appointed the local Justice of the Peace. I have only been doing this duty for three months. It's not hard. I act as a filter for the visiting Magistrate. For instance, if I had believed Tabu was possibly guilty of abetting a robbery, I would have referred his trial to the Magistrate and remanded him into custody.'

Michael said. 'It's probably good that you were on the bench today. Another Justice may have passed the decision to the Magistrate.'

Fred nodded 'Yes, perhaps. Maybe I have partly repaid my debt to him today.' He stood up ready to depart. 'Unfortunately, I am unable to stay. We're drenching sheep this week and I need to be there. I trust you will keep an eye on our friend and look out for him. Goodbye.' They each shook hands and went their separate ways.

Michael and Tabu headed the wagon out of Heathcote towards Kyneton via Redesdale on their way home. Michael suddenly started laughing, it was hard to believe how a simple act of help had caused so much concern and worry. Tabu did not understand why Michael was laughing. Michael did not try to explain.

They were now travelling through the district that they had last seen during the bushfire. The country side was tinged in green with the rolling hills showing evidence of new grass. Michael now fully understood the reason why the aboriginal tribes used to set fire to their land every five or six years. Fire would kill some wildlife but not all, they would continue to bred and the sun and rain would revitalise the grasslands and the life cycle would continue as it has done for countless centuries

Michael had become aware that Tabu was restless. Generally, he was stoic, expressionless and showed little interest in the country they travelled. Now that he was nearing his tribal land, he appeared restless. Michael knew that he would leave him soon. Michael only had the wagon, the spare horses, the dogs and two young rams to look after now and they were no trouble. The wagon was in good condition as were the animals. He did not need Tabu now to help with the droving, however he had been a good companion and Michael would miss having him around.

Without warning, one morning Tabu walked up to Michael and said 'I go now.'

Michael nodded and said 'If you need help from me, just come to the farm.'

Tabu picked up his possum skins and oddments turned and walked away. He stopped after walking for a few minutes, turned and waved, turned again and continued walking towards the distant hills. He knew he would find his tribe in the foothills. Michael knew he would see Tabu again one day.

Mandu was feeling old, he could see the changes in his body when he looked at the bodies of the young warriors. He rarely hunted now, although he had no need. As an elder he was tendered and fed by some lubras.

He often wondered where Tabu had gone. Mandu had asked other tribes to look out for him. He wanted to see him again as he felt his time was near. He sensed that Tabu would come in time. He felt that he was close by.

Tabu stood for a while looking down on the Yandarbee tribe camped on the banks of the Campaspe river. This was his tribe. Even though they were nomads, they didn't move very far. He had known that they would be easy to find.

The sun was high in the sky and the camp seemed almost deserted. The men would be out hunting and the women digging near the river's edge for roots. Only the old people and the children would be in the camp. The only sound was that of the yelping dogs.

He strode into the camp and sat in the middle of the mia mias. The dogs were still barking. The children were the first to see him. Some knew who he was. An old lubra walked over to him, looked at him then pointed to a tree under which a white-haired aborigine sat, with his head down.

A tribesman sat by his side looking at Tabu, he grabbed

the old man's arm and shouting he pointed. The old man was Mandu, his father. Tabu walked to his father and sat opposite him, neither spoke for a while. They both had their heads down.

Then Mandu looked up at him and said 'Tabu.'

Tabu nodded but did not speak.

Mandu then said 'Yu stay.' Tabu nodded and Mandu nodded in response.

'My Lubra she all go die, yu hunt me food?' asked Mandu.

Tabu nodded, stood up and walked away. He had been shocked to see how the once mighty warrior had changed in just a few years. He was sick with a white man's disease. Tabu decided that he would build a mia mia next to his father's.

The tribal members had gathered around Tabu, shouting and touching him, showing their delight at his return. He smiled acknowledging their welcome. Later that evening he joined their evening meeting circle. He told them of his travels and in return they told him of their lives during his absence.

Their lands were now being settled by the white men and it was difficult to hunt. The native animals had retreated further north. There was also the problem of the invading timber cutters, felling trees for planks and poles for farms and fences. The tribe was surviving but just. It was inevitable that their tribal lands would be lost. Tabu pondered, what of his tribe, where would they go? Other tribes would not welcome them. The future saddened him.

Tabu gradually settled into the tribal routine. Leaving early in the morning to hunt native wildlife or catching fish in crude vine nets or by spearing them. The warriors would return about noon, gut and skin their kills. Similarly, the lubras would go foraging for root plants and gathering seeds. When they returned to camp they were then required to cook the kills of the day. Tabu ensured his father was feed, although he ate little and was getting worse daily. Within two weeks of Tabu's return his father died.

His father was buried in the traditional way. The grieving by the tribal lubras reminded him of his brother's burial. Tabu mourned by himself. He had not been close to his father, but he still felt a gap had occurred in his life. Tribal life soon returned to normal and continued as before. His father's name would not be spoken again by any of the tribe's people. It was a tradition. Their term 'He die go along pinis' was apt for their culture.

At the start of each spring, when the flowers bloomed and the grass became green, several of the local tribes gathered together for a corroboree. Their corroboree dances imitated scenes such as hunting, a tribal battle or even copying a white man shearing.

This was also the time that a warrior would find his lubra. A tribe did not intermarry, generally only lubras from another tribe became a warrior's lubra. The lubra had no say in the matter. Sometimes young girls were promised at birth to a warrior. This was the case with Tabu. He knew that a young woman from the Wurundjeri tribe had been promised to him when he was a young boy. He had yet to meet her but when the time came and she was brought to him, he would accept her as his lubra. This was the tribal way.

The tribes would start to arrive for the corroboree over a period of several days and set up their camps a distance from the host tribe. Each then family immediately erected their mia mias and campfires.

The tribes then each sent an ambassador to meet with the host tribe, which this time was Tabu's tribe, the Yandarbee. The ambassadors came together at noon and sat a small way from the Yandarbee camp. After a short time, a warrior from Tabu's tribe went out and sat with them. They said little but agreed that the corroboree would be held in the evening in three days' time. They then rose and returned to their respective camps.

When the Yandarbee warrior had advised the tribes of the time for the corroboree, the men wander away to find the various ornaments that they would wear. The lubras began squealing and running to and fro showing their excitement for the coming event.

The warriors used burnt clay to mark their bodies and limbs, to present a fearsome skeleton design, around the eyes, across the ribs and down the legs. Each warrior's design was slightly different. Further adornment was added with possum skin strips tied around their head, upper arms and the waist. The waist band consisted of thick strips hanging at the front and the back. The adult lubras, not to be outdone, were adorned with wooden or shell combs in their hair and applied a fat compound to their faces.

The warriors without lubras, were camped a short distance from the main camp and were not permitted to socialise with the unattached women. They were left to their own interests.

The young girls to be mated, were in their early teens and sat quietly. No doubt apprehensive as to what their warrior would be like. They would soon know.

A flat area, adjacent the Yandarbee camp, had been cleared of brush and twigs for the corroboree. It had the appearance of a small arena. Large fires had been lit around the area. The visiting tribes who were to be spectators, now moved to the front of the arena.

The actual corroboree would be performed only by the host tribe. Their women would be in the background to provide the music, accompanied by didgeridoo players.

An Elder of the Yandarbee tribe stepped forward and directed the lubras to sit to the side and rear of the dance arena.

The lubras role was to chant while beating a rhythm on rolled possum skins held between their legs or slap their thighs.

All was ready. The night was quiet with only a few owls hooting in the distance and a few barking dogs. An Elder commenced proceedings by tapping two short thick sticks together, accompanied by didgeridoos giving out their pulsating and droning sounds. Immediately the lubras started to chant and screech and beat a rhythm. One by one the dancers emerged from the darkness behind the fires. Their slow running actions were synchronised. The dancers lined up in two rows. They each had a small shield and a spear.

The music slowly increased in tempo with the dancers appearing to be reaching a drugged state. The didgeridoos could be heard in the surrounding hills. Its mournful tone had a sound like no other. The fearsome look on the dancers' faces, their skeletal adornment and menacing attitude made a new spectator feel uncomfortable.

The dancers thumped their feet hard onto the ground raising puffs of dust, at the same time making a guttural sound with their voices. They continued to thump their feet harder and harder on the ground and becoming more agitated. In unison, the dancers performed several different moves. It soon became obvious that they were mimicking a tribal battle. They banged their spears on the shields, shouting and waving their arms in the air. They did this several times. The music reached a crescendo and the dancers poised as if to throw their spears and with a yell, they suddenly stopped. After a few seconds, the dancers walked from the arena, silently and with a dignified air, proud of their competence. All was quiet for a moment or so then the spectators started to talk excitedly with each other, indicating that they had enjoyed the corroboree.

The dancers reappeared, pleased with their performance and

chatted with their friends and other tribe members. If the other tribes liked this particular dance, they would probably copy the steps. The single warriors had enjoyed the corrorobee but they had other things on their minds. Tomorrow would be the day they claimed their lubras.

The next morning, as the Wurundjeri camp was stirring, a warrior named Jundi nudged his daughter and said to her 'Time yu go long Tabu yu longum him now.'

Bunga lay under possum skin and did not answer or even move. Her father kicked her lightly on her buttocks, repeating 'Wake now, yu go.'

Still she did not acknowledge him. Jundi walked to Bunga's mother and said 'Tell her go or I will hit her.' Her mother shrugged her shoulders and walked away.

Jundi had had enough, he picked up his club and went to Bunga and commanded once 'Get up — go now!' and when she did not move he hit her hard on the right shoulder. Bunga screamed but she did get up. She followed her father shuffling several steps behind him as they walked down to Tabu's camp.

Bunga had not seen Tabu before, but she had heard that he was the son of a senior Elder, who had died recently and that one day Tabu himself, would be an Elder. She knew he had been a drover for white men. She thought that he was an old man and had lubras already. If he had older lubras she would be doing all the work and would be beaten by them. The camp was not far, she could see the people were getting ready to go hunting. Her father spoke to a warrior who pointed to a mia mia on the edge of the camp.

Her father took her to the mia mia and called for Tabu.

Bunga heard a voice behind them say. 'I am Tabu.'

She kept looking to ground and heard her father say. 'This Bunga, lubra long yu.' Tabu saw a shy, wiry and strong young girl who had good skin and attractive features. Tabu was pleasantly surprised. He walked over to his mia mia, picked up two tomahawks and handed them to Jundi, who nodded to Tabu and walked away without saying a word to his daughter. Tabu put his hand on Bunga's shoulder. She winched and pulled away.

He said 'I not hurt yu.' He had unknowingly touched the shoulder that her father had hit with his club. Bunga looked up for the first time and saw a warrior who stood straight and tall.

She immediately thought 'He's not old.' She was less frightened now. She looked around and could not see any signs of other lubras.

Bravely she asked 'What lubra number me?'

Tabu looked at her, surprised at her question. 'Yu number one. Now yu go long other Lubras for food.' Bunga did as she was told.

The same 'marriage' event was occurring within the other tribes. Some young lubras were dragged to their new masters, while others were resigned to their fate. They might be crying but they did eventually accept their fathers' demand to go to their respective warriors. Immediately the lubras exchange was completed the tribes went their separate ways. The parents of the lubras seemed totally unconcerned as to their daughters' future, while the parents of the warriors seemed pleased to have another lubra in their family to share their tasks.

That morning, Tabu went hunting with the men but his mind was on his young lubra. He had been dreading the day she would arrive but now he was satisfied.

He had felt lonely for some time, perhaps now he would no longer go to the hill overlooking the camp and gaze out over the pasture lands below, watching the river flow and listening to the birds and their happy laughing sounds. He now had company.

The life of the Yandarbee tribe was becoming more difficult.

More and more settlers were arriving and the tribe was continually moving further north. Some clashes had occurred with neighbouring tribes because of them entering their tribal lands. All tribes were experiencing the same problem. This problem plus the diseases contracted from the white man were decimating most of them. Soon some tribes would cease to exist or the remainder would have no choice but to join with other similarly affected tribes to support each other. Their way of life was changing rapidly and would continue so forever.

In due course Bunga presented Tabu with a handsome young boy, who he called 'Jimmy'. One day he would take Bunga and Jimmy to meet Michael.

CHAPTER FIVE

Keogh or Somerset

Michael's homecoming was a mixture of tears and laughing. Mary could not stop smiling and asking him questions about the land that he had explored. Dinny also showed some emotion that his boss had returned safe and sound. The farm had been well maintained. The scene from the veranda, with the sheep grazing in the paddocks down to the river was as serene as ever, even though the grass was brown and dry. Little rain had fallen for the past few weeks with most of the days being hot and uncomfortable. However, the orchard and the vegetable gardens were all producing good quality marketable goods and being watered with tank water.

There was little for Michael to do around the farm. It was too dry to sow crops, the sheep had been crutched a few months ago and all the fences and sheds were in good order. Mary had tendered the garden and the small orchard with pride and joy. It was hers and hers only.

After a week, Michael became restless and needed to be occupied. He sat on the veranda and pondered. He recalled the questions Mary had asked when he first came home. During the evenings of his travels, he had made some notes of the country side, of the flora and fauna also the aboriginal habits he had seen. Was he capable of writing a book? Albeit — a report? Who would be interested, probably only the family. He decided, yes, he would do it.

He told Mary of his idea, who said jokingly but encouragingly. 'Yes, it will be better than having you moping around the farm doing nothing. It's a good idea. I think your experiences will be read with interest by other settlers looking for new land.'

Michael began to spend all his spare time writing what he could recall from memory and referencing his notes. The report took him nearly six months, with continuous additions as he continued to recall them as he refreshed his thoughts. Little did he realise the influence his report would have on his future.

The sun was relentless with its heat and north strong winds. There had hardly been a cloud in the skies for eight weeks. The normally green paddocks were now light brown, with dry long grass stalks which crunched underfoot, as you walked through the paddocks. The gum trees handled the heat well but many of the other trees had their leaves drooping. Some leaves had even shrivelled and dropped to the ground. Farms with limited water supplies had the farmers' wives giving up trying to keep their vegetables and flowers beds alive. Creeks and billabongs had dried up. Dams were becoming mud patches caused by the livestock trying to reach the diminishing water in the middle of the dams. Dead sheep were everywhere. Birds were falling dead from the tree branches. Farms, that had only added one water tank to help tide them over the bad times, were closely monitoring their level of water.

Most of the bigger farm houses that had installed water tanks, at several corners of their homesteads and their sheds, had sufficient drinking water available for many months. The local Campaspe river still had water flowing but it was very low. Dinny would tow a small sled with two water barrels up from the river to fill up the paddock water troughs for the livestock. The drought continued with no end in sight.

The Sunday sermon at each of the country churches was the same. It centred on the drought and the hardships the farmers faced now and after the drought was over and the courage they would need to see it through. The church congregation prayers were in earnest now and were no longer token prayers.

The loss of crops, death of calves and lambs, orchards with dead trees, had occurred before and the farmers had survived. It was this knowledge that kept them going and the belief that times would improve. It was just a matter of when?

At times the stress of providing for one's family caused severe friction between family members. The smallest problem could become a major issue and often with shouting and sometimes tears, in the good times the problem would have been forgotten in a moment. It was known that some farmers had committed suicide. Such was the level of the stress endured by the farming communities.

Tabu's Yandarbee tribe camped by the river under the gum trees and stayed there for the period of the drought. At night, they hunted possum, this was their main food. Occasionally they killed a kangaroo and the lubras managed to find some roots during their daily forages. Generally, they kept out of the sun and just sat around. The aborigines had been doing this since time immemorial. A little water plus a minimum supply of food had always successfully carried them through these ordeals. They were hardy people and had accepted their lot in life.

It was seven months before any meaningful rain fell and when it did, it was a deluge and continued unabated for two days. Roads were washed away. Coaches and bullock wagons were bogged. Trees were washed into the rivers and creeks and orchards flooded. But the drought was over — until next time. With their inherited optimism, the farmers were soon out in their paddocks again, sowing seed and grazing their livestock.

The Yandarbee tribe had left within the hour of the start of the rain and headed for the hilly country. They carried their arms, food and large sections of bark. Keeping to the east side of the ranges the tribe avoided the prevailing westerly winds and was sheltered from most of the rain. After a day's walk, they stopped in a small elevated open grass land in the lee of the mountain. Within an hour or so each family had erected a mia mia, had a fire lit, and started cooking. Life was normal again. There were caves within a short walk when the rains became too dense.

Both Michael's and John's farms had survived the full brunt of the drought but there had been some stock losses. The crops would be planted late and some of the orchard would have to be replanted again.

They both had a ready stock of dry fodder from the previous year so with any luck they might still have some fat cattle for sale in several months' time and hopefully the ewes would drop their lambs on time.

John's dams had been damaged by the heavy rainfall. The excess water had surged over and widened the cracks created by the drying sun. These cracks would be easily be repaired by John and Connor. They felled several trees and laid the branches close together and spread clay and brush between gaps and on top. This was soon compacted into a dam wall. They had been fortunate; other farmers would have to virtually start all over again.

Now that the drought had broken, John felt a sense of relief, knowing of the pressure on his friends who had struggled first through the drought and now the rain deluge. At times, he had felt guilty knowing he had survived the weather extremes in better condition than they had. He had made his troops available to help to support the community needs as requested by the Mayor's Office. The troops had repaired several priority roads and two bridges. John had now become entrenched in his position as the Senior Military Officer in the District and hence a recognised community leader.

The Mayor's secretary Carline Smith, was a local lass, most

efficient, too efficient at times. She came to John one morning with an open letter in her hand, she handed it to him saying. 'The Mayor thought that you should handle this matter.'

Under the letter's Official Heading, John read the following words:

> Office of the Mayor.
>
> Subject — Mr. Michael Somerset.
>
> Dear Sir,
>
> As a result of the recent local election we have discovered several discrepancies in the local residents register. We are unable to locate any record of a Mr Michael Somerset's arrival in the Colonies. He is listed as a rate payer in Kyneton and we are seeking an appropriate date or a ship's name for reference? We would appreciate, if you could use your good office to speak with Mr. Somerset on a personal basis. Your response to our query will enable my department to update our electoral rolls. Please treat this matter with a degree of urgency.
>
> Yours Faithfully.
>
> Peter Stephenson.
>
> Chief Electoral Officer

After all these years, how would Michael handle this news? What would be the effect on the family and his friends? Carline was looking at John waiting for his reaction. She knew Michael was his brother in law. She wondered if John knew of this matter and did he know the answer? John just sat in his chair thinking how best to handle this bombshell. He looked up and said 'Thank you.'

Carline sensed that there would be no immediate answer for the Mayor. She turned and went back to her office at the council chambers.

John donned his hat and coat and left the office. He needed to think. He strolled down the main street deep in thought, oblivious to everyone and everything. He eventually found himself in the newly established botanical gardens. Finding a seat under a shaded tree, he sat and pondered.

Michael was now a respected and wealthy sheep farmer. Should he advise him to go direct to the police and reveal his true identity? The days of transportation of convicts to the eastern colonies were now finished. Many of the convicts who had served out their sentences had become responsible members of the community. Surely Michael's contribution to the local community over many years would be recognised. However, the fact remained that he was still an escaped convict.

The other option would be to create a falsehood. But that would not solve the problem. Michael would spend the rest of his life wondering if he would eventually be located and be identified as an escaped convict. John decided to see Michael and advise him of the letter's contents and to sit with him, to help him make a decision.

Michael saw John approaching the farm house and waved to him from the vine covered veranda. For ten years the vines had been growing along the veranda bearers and now they covered nearly all of the wooden frames. When the vines bloomed, it was a magnificent sight. He often had lunch there, shaded by the vines.

Michael asked 'What brings you out this way? We normally only see you on weekends.' He could see that John was not his cheerful self.

'Unfortunately, I have bad news which you and I need to talk about.'

Michael nodded and said. 'Come inside and we can talk over a cup of tea.'

He called the maid and asked her to bring tea to the study.

John answered, saying 'Read this letter first and then we can talk.'

Michael read the letter and then stood up and walked around the room. He was shocked. He did not say a word.

John spoke first saying 'You have two options. One — you go to the police. Two — you can create a falsehood. Personally, I would go to the police and have the situation resolved regardless of the consequences.'

Michael stood deep in thought. He said 'In the back of my mind I have always had this fear. I guess it had to come to this one day. What of Mary if I'm gaoled?'

'It may not get to that but even if you were gaoled, we would be here to support her. Your immediate concern is for yourself. Think about it over the next day or so then let me know your decision and we can talk again' replied John.

Michael nodded and sat down, tea had arrived and they changed the subject and began talking about their crops for the coming summer.

After John left, Michael went looking for Mary to advise her of the unwelcome news. Mary sat there listening to her husband. She had been aware that Michael was an escaped convict but she had not considered that he would be found out, particularly after all these years.

Outwardly she was calm but inwardly she was terrified that she would lose Michael. For Michael to be gaoled was unthinkable in her eyes. When she spoke she chose her words with care. She said. 'You will always be my husband, come what may. I'll be here.'

The next few days were a torment for Michael. What should he do! He had to consider Mary in his decision. He walked down the small hill to the river bank. John was right he had two options or three, what if he left the farm and went north, but this was unthinkable. The farm was their home. Finally, he decided he would surrender himself to the police. When he told Mary, she broke down, cried and then hugged him.

'I know that you have made the right choice' she said between sobs.

Michael said 'I'll see John next week and get his advice on how best to go about it.'

John had already anticipated that Michael would surrender himself and had quietly made enquiries about Michael's situation. He was surprised to find that other convicts had come forward and, depending upon their current community status, most had been exonerated.

The Abolitionists had made a good case to the Colonial Secretary for the cessation of Transportation of Convicts to the eastern colonies. The reports of the brutal history of Norfolk Island, Port Arthur and finally the killing of Superintendent Price on the hulk 'Success' in Hobson's Bay were prime evidences submitted in their case. The subsequent investigation revealed that the current penal system was inhuman, outmoded and unacceptable in the current social climate.

John had investigated the methods and the reasons that had been used successfully in supporting a case for leniency, in the cases of escaped convicts, through a discreet enquire with a recently retired Magistrate who now lived in Kyneton.

Michael and Mary arrived at John and Maeve's farm for their monthly Sunday lunch. They visited each other's farm month and month about. They had been doing it for several years. It was now a ritual. The women went to the kitchen talking about everything and nothing. Michael accompanied John into study where they both sat down, facing each other.

John started 'Have you made a decision yet?'

Michael replied 'Yes I'll surrender to the police, it's the best in the long run, I don't want to be waiting for a knock on the door until the day I die.'

John nodded 'For what it's worth, I think that's the correct decision.' He continued. 'I've made some discrete enquiries and you will not be the first escaped convict who has surrendered to the police.'

Michael was surprised at this comment and was about to speak but John put up his hand. Saying 'Let me finish. Most have been exonerated, not all but most. So we should be optimistic. We need to do a few things first and quickly before you go to the police. I suggest we allow three to four weeks to get the following documents.'

John continued:-

'One — We will need a copy of the transcript of your trial in Ireland. This will be in the Port Arthur files.

Two — A copy of your file from the Port Arthur Prison Superintendent's records.

Three — A copy of the Abolitionist Submission to the British Parliament together with a copy of the Colonial Secretary's Report.

Four — Character references. Even from me as a Military Officer, a Justice of the Peace and several local community Identities.

Five — Locate a sympathetic Magistrate, hopefully a farmer himself. If we can identify one, perhaps we can delay the hearing to match his scheduled visit, by saying we are awaiting supporting documents. This may be difficult and even unnecessary.'

He paused. 'Finally, you will need to write a report to the Magistrate detailing your current status together with your contribution to the community. Ignore anything to do with your escape.' John stopped talking.

Michael finished writing down the suggestions. Michael was

all smiles 'That's good, at least I know I have a chance of exoneration and don't forget my Tasmanian friend, George Alford, he's a Justice of the Peace and a Shire President.'

The discussion finished there as the women announced. 'Lunch is ready to be served!'

Mary drove the gig home while Michael sat deep in thought about what John had suggested. It was all logical and made sense. He glanced at Mary and blessed his good fortune to have married a woman with her attributes. Their farm was prospering, because of her knowledge and enthusiasm to try new ideas with the garden produce. She could cook, sew and make him feel appreciated as his partner in life. Together with John's help they would survive this trial of their life.

Michael sat with a pen in hand, thought for a moment and then started to write about his involvement in local community life and his success as a farmer. He had been a drover for many of the older farmers in the district who were unable to stand the long hours on horseback and being away from their farms for any length of time. When his shearing partner Seamus had been alive, they had established a name as good and honest shearers. He knew he was respected by the other farmers and was hopeful they would continue to respect him when they found out that he was an escaped Irish convict. There were many farmers and labourers around the district who were from County Clare and other West Ireland Counties.

He felt that they would be supportive. Indeed, some were ex-convicts themselves. He continued writing, between thinking, for many hours. He had started his letter by writing how he had been taught to shear. How he and Seamus went from farm to farm seeking work and during that time they saved enough money to purchase their property and rebuilt the remains of a stone cottage. How they established a small flock of sheep and improved the stock line, the starting of a vegetable garden and orchard and with their produce being sold in Bendigo and Kyneton at the local markets.

He decided to write of his recent droving trip, through areas of Victoria which few white men had seen. Michael was not to know, but the Magistrate he was destined to stand before was a member of a Government Board tasked to identify the grazing prospects of land in the Victorian area between the Murray River and the town of Heathcote, a 100 miles south of the river. The Government wished to subdivide the area for settlement. This was the area through which the explorer Major Michael had travelled.

Michael's description of the grasslands, forests and water availability would answer many of the questions that the Government was seeking. He may not have been the first person to view the area but he would be the first to describe it in detail in a written report to an official of the Government.

Michael had not lost contact with George Alford, they exchanged a few letters each year. He had only written to him a month ago, so George was surprised to receive another letter so soon. He read the letter with interest and could not believe Michael's bad luck after all of these years.

Michael had explained that his requested letter would be presented to the Magistrate to support a case of leniency. Yes, George would supply him with a letter of character reference, even after all these years.

The second request needed some thought. To obtain a copy of Michael's trial transcript and the prison commandant's report on him, would not be easy. John had written to Mr George Walter C/- The Tasmanian Government Administration Dept. Hobart. George Walters was a former marine officer who John had met on on-board ship when he had first travelled to Melbourne from

England. He knew George had left the marines and joined the Tasmanian Government but John didn't know in what capacity? John asked George if he had any influence or contacts to enable him to obtain copies of Michael's trial transcript and prison report.

George Walters had not heard from John for nearly a year and was pleasantly surprised to receive the letter. He was employed as the Supervisor of the Government Administration staff. Although not directly responsible for the Government Archives, he had some authority in the area, by providing staff. As John's letter indicated a level of urgency, he started to explore the best avenue to locate the documents without raising any undue concerns.

Port Arthur documents were kept in a dungeon under the Customs House near the wharf, and were looked after by Fred Green, an old ex-convict sentenced for forgery. Fred's main job was to arrange the filing of government data and also to protect the files from being damage by damp, vermin and whatever. He had kept the job for many years because, apart from being educated, he had an excellent memory and knew the exact location of most of the respective Government's Departmental records. George knew him quite well, as he had needed Fred's help several times in the past to locate specific office records.

George asked him if he could locate Michael Keogh's trial transcript and prison records from his Port Arthur's time during 1853 and to be discreet.

Fred nodded and said 'Give me two days Sir; I will need to move about fifty boxes.'

Two days later when George returned to the dungeon, Fred stepped forward and handed him the trial transcript.

Saying 'The prison reports are not here, I think they are in the main Government building.'

'How sure are you?' asked George.

Fred shrugged his shoulders and walked away. George had his scribe copy the transcript and then returned the original document to Fred.

The head of George's Department was a former Port Arthur Penal Commandant. On his retirement from that position he had been offered the position of Superintendent of the Tasmanian Civil Service. George had no choice but to meet him and so made an appointment with his office. He had to wait two days due to the Superintendent's other commitments.

The Superintendent's clerk usher George into his office. He stood up and came around the desk to shake George's hand and then returned to his chair, motioning George to be seated.

Saying 'My apologies Walters that I couldn't see you sooner, business you know. What can I do for you?' George took a deep breath, he was on good terms with his Superintendent, but this might test his faith in him.

'I have an unusual request from a friend of mine in Victoria. He knows of a person, an ex-convict who wishes to surrender to the police.'

The Superintendent said 'After all these years I thought that business was behind us, but continue, how can I help you?'

'He wants to present his prison record to the Magistrate to enhance his plea for leniency. It's possible his records are held here by your department' George paused, waiting for the Superintendent's reaction.

'Yes, go on.' The Superintendent asked. He was listening intently.

'Would it be possible to obtain a copy of them?' asked George.

'It's an unusual request but yes, I could agree to that. What is the convict's name?'

George replied 'Michael Keogh.'

The Superintendent came from behind his desk again and

sat down next to George, saying 'Good God, after all of these years. Did you know he and his colleague Seamus Lynch were the only two convicts to escape from Port Arthur when I was the Commandant?'

'In a way, I was partly responsible. I remember that I told him he would not be released until I had a replacement shipwright and that I had no idea when that would be. They escaped two weeks later. I should never have told him.' He paused 'Do you know where he is?'

'In all honesty, no' answered George. He had not been told these facts.

The Supervisor sat deep in thought. He looked at George and said. 'Yes, it's been a long time since those dark days. I have no objection. He can have a copy of his prison record and I hope it assists in his pardon. I'll have my clerk arrange the copy, see him in future'

George stood up, thanked his Superintendent and left his office. He was unsure of the tone of the meeting but he was satisfied with its result. The document was located the next day, duly copied and handed to George. Within three days John's request had been fulfilled. A letter with the documents was on its way from Hobart and reached Kyneton within the week.

Both John and Michael were in debt to George Walters for his speedy efforts. When John received the letters, he rode immediately to Michael's farm and handed them to him. Both sat down and eagerly read the prison report. It was significant by the fact that it had only routine comments about him, other than his escape, indicating that Michael had not caused trouble during his term at Port Arthur. The trial transcript was accurate and it was obvious to any who read the document that Michael had been grossly mistreated which was indicative of the legal system in those terrible times.

The trial transcript read — *Michael Keogh is charged with*

— Interfering with the lawful duties of a constable in that he grabbed hold of a bridle and caused the horse to unseat the constable. Nothing was written as to why Michael had grabbed the bridle — he had been protecting a mother, holding a baby, from the rearing horse.

John and Michael sat down to think of what other ways could there be to enhance Michael's chances of a pardon by the Crown? They now possessed as exhibits:-

1 A copy of the transcript of Michael's trial in Ireland.

2 A copy of Michael's prison record from Port Arthur..

3 A letter of support from a Senior Victorian Military Officer

4 A letter of support from George Alford J.P. and also a Shire President of long standing.

5 Four Character references from local business community leaders.

6 A letter written by Michael detailing who he was and his reason for writing the letter. He then went on to state his contribution to the colony as a successful farmer and his community involvement.

7 His experience as a drover/explorer. (He added the report as an attachment to the letter, which included the maps he had made of the district and his dealings with the aborigines and what he had learnt from Tabu.)

8 His final paragraph included his request to be heard by a Magistrate to plea his case as 'An escaped convict' for exoneration and a pardon by the Crown.

9 The Abolitionists submission and the Colonial Secretaries answer.

They decided that they had sufficient documents to support Michael's application for exoneration and a pardon from the Crown. Michael sat down and wrote a short note to the Magistrate of the Kyneton Court. The note stated who he was and why he was submitting the package. Michael attached the note to the front of the exhibits and placed them in an envelope and then rode into Kyneton.

He sat on his horse in front of the court house for a few minutes. He knew that once he handed over the envelope he was committed to stand before the Magistrate. He dismounted and walked to the counter and handed over the envelope to the clerk. Who nodded to Michael and then placed it in a tray marked 'Magistrate.' Michael turned and walked out feeling very apprehensive.

A letter arrived three weeks later. The letter acknowledged receipt of the documents together with a second letter requiring Michael to attend court to answer a charge of 'Escaping from Lawful Custody' The hearing was scheduled to be in two weeks' time at the Kyneton court house.

The Magistrate would be James Hogan who was not known in the local district. He had only recently moved to Melbourne after spending several years in the western district. So possibly he was a farmer? Michael's immediate future would be decided by a total stranger but at least he was from a farming area. No doubt he would appreciate that the future of the colony would be in the prosperity of the rural areas.

Michael and Mary arrived at the court house in a gig. As he tethered the horse, John and Maeve arrived. The district had soon become aware of Michael's pending court hearing and a crowd had assembled waiting for the court house doors to open. It appeared most of the locals were interested in Michael's future. Several friends walked over to Michael and wished him luck.

Michael tried to hide his concern regarding the decision from Mary. He could see that she was anxious by the way she was nervously twisting her handkerchief. The court house doors opened and the ground floor seats were soon filled. John took

Maeve and Mary up to the balcony and obtained front row seats which were almost above the front seats of the ground floor and were looking down onto the witness box.

The Clerk of Courts walked into the courtroom carrying several paper files, he placed them on his desk, turned to the court visitors, paused and then said 'All rise'.

The Magistrate walked to the bench, bowed to the court and then took his seat.

The congregation then noisily sat down. Michael had been taken to a seat close to the witness stand.

'The Kyneton Court is now in session, Magistrate Hogan presiding.

The Crown versus Michael Keogh who is charged with 'Escaping from lawful custody" read the Clerk.

'Michael Keogh please take the stand.'

Michael walked positively to the stand and stood straight and tall. He was smartly dressed, well-groomed and had a commanding presence. One wondered, how could this man have been a convict?

The Clerk handed Michael a bible and asked 'Do you swear to tell the truth and nothing but the truth?'

Michael responded. 'I do.'

'How do you plea?' asked the clerk

Michael responded firmly 'Guilty.'

The Clerk collected the bible and then sat down. The trial was now set to begin.

The Magistrate was a tall man and he sat very upright. He had the posture of an ex-cavalry officer. He had a strong jaw and you could sense his confidence.

He looked directly at Michael and said 'How you answer my questions today will decide your future, so please ensure that you think before you respond, is that clear?'

Michael returned his look and thought at least I will get a fair hearing. 'I fully understand Your Honour' said Michael in a strong clear voice.

The Magistrate asked 'To the best of your knowledge are these exhibits true and correct?'

Michael could see each of the documents that he had forwarded with his submission on the table and answered without hesitation 'Yes.'

The Magistrate continued 'I have read all of the exhibits.

First. I am familiar with the Abolitionists submission and the Colonial Secretary's response. With which I agree.

Second. You have the support of several respected community leaders. Very good.

Third. The transcript of your trial is of interest.'

Michael's heart skipped a beat or two, when he heard this comment. This was the crux of the hearing or so he thought.

The Magistrate continued. 'You no doubt broke the law by Quote 'Interfering with the lawful duties of a constable in that Michael Keogh grabbed hold of the bridle of a constable's horse and caused the horse to unseat the constable.' Unquote. However, I believe that the sentence imposed was inappropriate for the offence. This offence would be viewed differently nowadays and would only incur a minor penalty, possibly only a fine.'

'Fourth. Your prison record has no entries of offences during your imprisonment. However, you did break the law by escaping from lawful custody. I'll come back to that.'

You could sense an air of foreboding in the Court when the magistrate said these words.

'Your letter concerning your life, since your escape, makes for interesting reading.' He looked at Michael. 'You have progressed and improved your lot in life over the past years. I would have thought you would have married' commented the Magistrate.

'But I am Your Honour!' interrupted Michael.

'Mr. Keogh. That fact should have been your first exhibit! Marriage indicates stability and responsibility. This is what we look for in cases like yours. Is your wife here today?'

Michael turned and pointed to the balcony. 'She is sitting up there.'

Mary blushed and lowered her head. The Magistrate nodded and said 'Thank you, do you wish to add or say anything more to your submission?'

Michael thought for a moment or two. He answered 'No, Your Honour.'

'You may return to your seat Mr. Keogh,' said Magistrate Hogan.

The Clerk whispered to the Magistrate, who nodded. The Clerk turned and said 'The Court will convene for one hour. All rise.' After much shuffling and scraping of chairs on the floor, the court emptied.

Michael found John and the two women waiting outside the court house for him. John suggested that they adjourn to the Royal Hotel for lunch. After a short walk, they were soon seated in a corner of the dining room. Little was said until their orders had been taken.

John started saying 'Well there have been no real negatives so far, I feel comfortable that you will receive a reasonable decision.'

Michael did not answer; he was concerned with the comment made by the Magistrate about 'coming back to that.' Mary and Maeve said nothing, as both were reluctant to comment.

Michael eventually said 'I think John is correct, we will soon know. Let's make sure that we're not late back to the court house.'

They arrived with five minutes to spare. The seats were all occupied except for their seats. They had been left vacant.

Michael was nervous and returned to the witness box without being asked and sat down.

On the hour, the Clerk walked to the front of the court and called 'All rise.'

After the Magistrate was seated, the clerk said 'The Court is now in session, Magistrate Hogan presiding.'

'I have spent the recess hour re-reading the events of your past several years and I see that you have recently been droving in northern Victoria up around the Major's Line. How long did you spend there?' asked the Magistrate.

Michael replied 'I was away from home for around three months. I spent around two months between Heathcote, Tongala and the Murray River around Echuca.'

The Magistrate said 'Your description and maps are the most comprehensive reports I have seen on this area of the colony and it is pleasing to see your unbiased report on the local aborigines. The Government would be most interested in its contents.'

'Mr. Keogh before I summarise this case, this is your last chance to present any other exhibits or comments that you may wish to offer in your support?' asked the Magistrate.

Michael thought for a while; was their anything else to support his case for a Pardon? What more could be said, he and John had discussed the situation time and time again.

He answered 'No, Your Honour.'

The Magistrate commenced reading 'There is no doubt that Mr. Keogh has led an exemplary life for the last sixteen years and he has achieved the status of a successful farmer, drover and a respected member of the community. His droving exploits will benefit the colony and those who will eventually settle the lands in the north of Victoria. It is also acknowledged that his sentence is out of all proportion for his crime.

These days the offence would be regarded as minor.

Furthermore, I believe that Mr. Keogh would have served out his sentence and ultimately been entitled to his freedom. Unfortunately, his unique skills as a boat builder required the authorities to keep him at the Port Arthur Penal settlement, as they had no replacement, thus denying him a probationary release period. This prompted him to plan and execute his escape.'

He paused and then said. 'This being an unlawful act.' The Magistrate stopped.

Michael was stunned. He thought he would be exonerated.

'Mr. Keogh Please stand.' said the Magistrate.

Michael stood and gripped the witness stand rail with both hands.

The Magistrate continued. 'Michael Keogh I find you guilty of escaping from lawful custody and I sentence you to the 'Rising of the court' and that no conviction be recorded. Further, that Mr. Keogh is pardoned from completing the remainder of his sentence for the crime of 'Interference with the lawful duties of a constable'. Quote In that he grabbed the bridle causing the horse to unseat the constable Unquote.'

The Magistrate nodded to the clerk, who stood up and called 'All rise.' The Magistrate stood up then bowed and left the court room.

The court room erupted into loud cheering and applause. Michael stood there for a moment absorbing what had happened.

The clerk walked over to him and said 'You are free to go. You will receive the appropriate discharge papers within a few weeks. Also, the Magistrate wishes to talk with you regarding the 'Major's Line' report before you go.'

Michael sat down in the witness box staring into space. He was legally free at last, after all of these years, being mindful over his past.

He heard a voice saying 'Michael! Michael! It's over.' It was Mary with tears streaming from her eyes. He stood up and held her in his arms.

John was patting him on the back. Maeve was also crying standing alongside John.

Other friends of Michael's were shouting 'Well done,' 'Hurrah.'

The Clerk of the Court was standing back waiting to catch Michael's eye. Michael nodded to him.

He said 'You can bring your family.' The Clerk then led them into the Magistrate's office.

Magistrate Hogan stood up and greeted them with a handshake and invited them to be seated. He then explained that apart from being appointed the District Magistrate for this area, he had been tasked to evaluate the farming and grazing value and to advise the best way to sub-divide these northern Victorian lands, in which Michael had been travelling.

He continued saying 'Your maps and description of the soil, water and foliage as well as the aborigines, make you an expert on the area.'

Michael wondered where this conversation was heading. He had been curious when the Magistrate queried him in the court about his knowledge of the north Victorian district.

The Magistrate looked at Michael and said 'I'll be brief, I have to be in Bendigo by midday tomorrow and I must leave as soon as possible. Another of my many roles in the Victorian Government requires me to identify persons who could be considered to be appointed as Commissioners of Crown Lands. The colony needs to start controlling land ownership and titles of country properties, particularly in the areas more remote from Melbourne.'

He continued 'You are an experienced, well-travelled drover

and farmer who is obviously educated and well respected plus you have written an excellent detailed report of the Northern district. We need people like you to help open up this district in a controlled and legal manner. You are one of these persons who could be considered for one of these positions. I would like you to think about it for week or so. It will not be an easy job but it's a very important one for the future of our colony. If you are interested in further discussions with me, regarding this position, please contact the Clerk, and I will forward details of the position to you. You can always contact me by leaving a message at the court house.'

He looked at the clock on the wall and said. 'I'm sorry but I must go now, good bye.'

After a hurried exchange of farewells, Michael and John left the court house with their wives and headed home. Michael sat quietly in the gig thinking of his extraordinary change of fortune. Not only had he been exonerated but he had been offered a senior Government position.

Driving home in the gig, Mary said 'What is our name now, is it Somerset or Keogh? Our marriage certificate says it is Somerset but your birth name is Keogh. That will now go on the electoral roll.' Michael nodded and thought maybe I should change my name to Somerset for the electoral roll. Their property, bank accounts, marriage certificate, rates, livestock brands, mail and other minor items all used Somerset as the family name.

Yes, he would change his name to Somerset. Michael Keogh was now in the past. After a long discussion, they decided that if they had children, the first child would be called Keogh Somerset regardless of the child's gender.

CHAPTER SIX

The Commissioner

The thought of being a Commissioner of Crown Lands was attractive to Michael, he had always enjoyed the open-air life and if he could help the new colony become of age, well and good. Perhaps his bush and country town life experience could help him to help others. He felt he owed the colony something in return for his good fortune and this position could be his way of payment. He decided to meet with Magistrate Hogan to further discuss the position and its responsibilities.

However, Mary was concerned about the amount of time Michael would be away. Mary was now thirty-eight years of age and believed that she was pregnant. She would know within two weeks' time when she was to visit Dr Post. She was worried now that Michael would not be near to support her in her pregnancy if he took the position. Even though Maeve was only a few miles away, she really wanted Michael to be with her.

Michael duly wrote to Magistrate Hogan requesting an audience. He promptly received an answer requiring him to attend a meeting with him at his office in the Melbourne court house at noon in four days' time. Michael was more curious than apprehensive about the possibility of him being appointed a Commissioner of Crown Lands. He looked forward to the meeting.

The day before the meeting, he rode to the Kyneton Cobb & Co. office, leaving his horse at their stables and boarded their stagecoach to Melbourne. He stayed with a friend in Collingwood that evening and caught up with the Melbourne gossip. The next morning he hired a Hansom Cab to drive him to the court house. The three mile jaunt allowed him to see the development of Melbourne. It was an untidy town with potholes in the roads, some full of water but he could see some private bluestone buildings of note. Cathedrals, government buildings and several banks had also been erected. These buildings would stand for a long time. He predicted that one day Melbourne would be a large and important city and be known throughout the world.

The Melbourne court house was imposing. The uniform doorman had him listed as a visitor and smartly escorted him to a waiting room.

Within minutes Magistrate Hogan appeared smiling. 'Welcome to Melbourne Mr Keogh. We can talk in my office.'

Michael walked alongside the Magistrate, admiring the internal design of the passageway. They turned and entered a well-appointed office. Michael was further impressed and said so. Magistrate Hogan replied that this building was built to last and to portray the importance and authority of the Law Department to the public.

They sat down opposite each other with only a small low table between them.

Michael felt comfortable and was aware of effort the Magistrate was making to ensure a relaxed interview.

After they had a few casual words, the Magistrate started the interview by asking 'What does your wife think of this possible appointment?'

Michael had expected him to ask him for his thoughts first. He answered 'She is uncertain as we don't have sufficient knowledge of the commitment required from me as yet.'

'Excellent, an open mind is good. I would have had concerns if she had made up her mind at this stage.' The Magistrate continued 'Briefly, the position requires on the spot decisions regarding boundaries of claims in districts yet to be officially surveyed or have been surveyed poorly, and to issue licenses to allow the applicants to settle on the land long term and to begin grazing his livestock or whatever he wishes to farm or bred. Many have already become 'Squatters' and as you are no doubt aware most boundaries are marked by tree blazing with an axe cut and a cross or initial etc. Sometime markers are erected but these are easily removed. Few claimants still do this now. River boundaries are popular as they are definitely permanent. Very few roads or tracks will remain as they are. The properties will need to be surveyed and registered to have any legality. A Commissioner's decision can be challenged and maybe overturned but in the interim period, we need Commissioners or we will have anarchy.'

He paused. 'Apart from the Land control issue, Commissioners have the authority and the responsibility for deciding the issuance and renewal of public house licenses and the prices of the publicans' services and charges. They may also be asked to adjudicate in minor disputes, such as stock ownership, water rights and access etc. They have lawful authority with limitations. Commissioners may request support from the police and often when they go into new territory, they take two or three armed constables with them.'

He pointed to a map on the wall. 'An office would be provided for a Commissioner at the Kyneton police barracks and their horses would be available to him. Well, I've done enough talking. Do you have any questions?'

Michael had listened intently and he liked what he had heard. It sounded not only interesting but challenging. He asked the question which he knew Mary would ask. 'How long do these district visits normally take?'

The Magistrate replied 'Generally two to three weeks. A lot of ground can be covered in this time. As you know a good horse can cover up to fifty miles in a day or eighty in two days on good country tracks. If you halve these distances you can still cover a large area within this time. As Commissioner you would plan the area you would wish to cover, allowing yourself sufficient time for your visit.'

The Magistrate added 'On return to the barracks office, your reports would be required to be completed together with maps of the district and the boundaries agreed, and with whom. Naturally, other decisions or commitments made to citizens would also be subject to separate reports. These would be forwarded to my office. Do you have any other questions?'

Michael said 'No, I need to have a think about the commitment required. But, I am very interested. I would like to talk to my wife and then advise you of my decision. Is that agreeable to you?'

'Yes, and I will look forward to your decision. If you are interested, I would like you to fill in this form with your personal details and forward it to me, it is self-explanatory. We would then talk further and discuss any queries you may have,' replied the Magistrate, they both stood up and shook hands.

Michael said 'I should like you to know that I will be changing my family name to 'Somerset'. This is the name I have been using for many years with my day to day activities, our marriage and our paperwork.'

The Magistrate nodded his understanding. He then walked Michael to the court house entry and said 'I hope we meet again.' They shook hands. He then turned and went back inside the building.

Michael stood there for a while deep in thought, before walking down to the Cobb& Co. stagecoach office to head back to Kyneton that afternoon. Mary saw Michael riding up the carriageway. She hadn't told him of the possibility that she was pregnant yet and she would not until she was sure. She walked down from the veranda and waved to him. He waved back smiling. Michael quickly dismounted and after kissing her he put his arm around her and together they walked to the stables, where he handed the reins of the horse to Dinny for him to unharness.

Arm in arm they walked to the orchard shade house and sat down looking at each other. Mary was dreading what he was going to say. But she would support his decision.

Mary started the conversation and asked 'Well, what do you have to tell me about the meeting?'

Michael spoke quietly and slowly and repeated everything that Magistrate Hogan has said. Mary sat quietly listening and absorbing Michael's words. Michael then waited for her to reply.

Mary nodded 'I can see that you are thinking of accepting the position. At least you can decide when you need to go, and two to three weeks is not so long. You're away that long when you go shearing.' She felt satisfied. If she was pregnant Michael could stay home and be with her.

Michael listened to her and stared down the paddock to the river. He was thinking, would Mary tell him the truth if she did not want him to take the job?

He moved to her and put his arms around her and said 'Let us think about it for a few days and then we can make a decision.' They walked back to the farmhouse in the moonlight, again arm in arm.

The next few days Michael kept himself busy. He and Dinny walked around the fences and repaired them as necessary. Kangaroos were continually hitting them when hopping across the paddocks. They could jump high but not when travelling fast. They were prone to misjudge the jump and hit the fence wires, sometimes breaking the wooden posts. Often the kangaroos were badly injured and had to be shot.

That night he sat on the porch looking down to the river and the sunset. It was a spectacular sight when the sun was low and the sky was red. He wanted to take the position or at least — give it a go. If it did not suit him or vice versa he could always resign. Mary was quiet, she knew he was trying to make up his mind and thought it better not to interrupt his ponderings. She sat inside knitting a small pink and blue shawl. Michael did not realise the significance of her knitting, only a woman would.

Michael had soon made his decision. He called Mary to come to the porch. She delayed the discussion deliberately by making tea. She eventually come to the porch and after giving Michael a cup of tea she sat down, straightened her dress then looked directly at Michael and said 'Well!'

'I would like to accept the position. I can always resign if either of us is unhappy with my absences.' Michael waited for Mary to comment.

She sat there silently looking at Michael. 'Yes, I agree. I can see you would like to be a Commissioner and as you say if either of us is unhappy, you can resign. Regardless, I think you must take the position or you will always wonder — what if.'

Michael stood up walked to Mary, leant over and kissed her and said 'I was blessed when I met you.' He sat down alongside her, both of them enjoying the sunset.

The next morning Michael completed the application form and wrote a letter advising Magistrate Hogan of his wish to formally apply for a position as a Commissioner of Lands. He then rode into the Kyneton stagecoach office to post the letter and the form. He decided to the walk past the police barracks. It was a small blue stone building with large stables at the rear and a paddock alongside. He thought, I may soon see inside it as a government official. A week later a letter arrived requesting him to present himself to the Magistrate Hogan's office again.

He arrived in Melbourne and was at Magistrate Hogan's office at noon. He was ushered in by him and then introduced to two other men. They were introduced as the Chief Magistrate and the State Records Superintendent. They sat in a circle and tea was served.

The Chief Magistrate spoke first saying 'I have read your details and I am most impressed with your knowledge of the Northern Victorian district. Your reports will greatly assist in helping the Surveying teams. Wouldn't you agree?' He looked at the Superintendent. 'Yes, you are correct Sir, the maps are of particular interest and your reports on the aborigines should help us. Our police force need to better understand them and their cultural values. There is no doubt that our different cultures will be difficult to bridge. Incidentally, do you have any more reports on the district? The ones you supplied are now part of our official records.'

Michael shook his head and replied 'Sorry, but no.'

The Chief Magistrate then nodded to Magistrate Hogan

Magistrate Hogan asked 'Before we proceed further, do you have any questions?'

Michael replied 'I think I have a good appreciation of the duties but obviously I lack procedural experience which I trust I will acquire with training.'

Magistrate Hogan nodded saying 'We have examined your credentials and have spoken with people who have had dealings with you and together with our knowledge of your bush experience, we are satisfied with your suitability for the position and yes, training would be provided. Subsequently, we are prepared to formally offer you a position as a Commissioner of Crown Lands. Your remuneration and expense entitlements are detailed on this form.' Michael looked at the form and then back at the Magistrate. Who asked. 'Do you accept the position?'

Michael could hardly contain himself with delight. He smiled and said 'Yes Sir.'

They all stood up and the Chief Magistrate shook Michael's hand saying 'Welcome aboard Mr. Somerset.'

The Superintendent and Magistrate Hogan each shook his hand and congratulated him and wished him well in his new role. The Chief Magistrate and the Superintendent then left the room.

Magistrate Hogan called his Clerk to come into the office and motioned Michael to follow him.

He was then sworn in as an Officer of the Court. The duties and responsibilities accompanying the position were restated together with the reporting procedures to be observed. Michael was then handed a procedures manual and a brief which detailed the legal requirements of land title registration.

Magistrate Hogan said 'I would like you to report back to me within two weeks and spend some time here at the courts. This will give you an in-depth background to our work and also give you the chance to meet with our other Commissioners and receive some training. We have eight at this moment. Some are based here. Finally, I will send you some documents for you to view. You will need to sign them.'

Michael was impressed with the no nonsense approach each of the men had.

They were direct and positive. Michael and the Magistrate then proceeded to the court house dining room, where they had the chance to get to know each other better. It was obvious that the Magistrate was Michael's senior officer. Michael stood when the Magistrate did. He shook his hand, thanked him for lunch and said that he looked forward to reporting for duty within two weeks. He turned and left the court house. He was almost cheering — Commissioner Michael Somerset — unbelievable.

When he reached Kyneton, he went to the George Inn and had a few ales to relax. He was still excited. He sat chatting with some friends but said nothing regarding his new position. He wanted Mary to be the first know. He left after an hour and headed home, whistling all the way, the ales probably contributing towards his elation.

He called Mary, who he could see down in the orchard picking fruit. She walked up, hugged and kissed him, took his hand and led him to the porch.

They sat down. Mary looked at him and said 'Well! What happened'? Michael was smiling. She continued 'By the smile on your face, I presume that you have been made a Commissioner.'

Michael nodded and answered 'Yes, I have to go back in two weeks' time to finalise the paperwork.'

He paused. 'Don't worry, you will always come first. I would like to share the news with John and Maeve this weekend during Sunday lunch at their farm.'

Mary nodded, she knew that they always had a Sunday roast meat lunch and two unannounced visitors dropping in would not be a problem for them to be included at their table.

John saw the gig approaching and recognised the passengers. He waved and went to meet them. He called out to Maeve 'We have visitors for lunch, come and see.'

Connor walked out from the stables and took the reins from Michael as John helped Mary alight. They hugged and shook hands. The two families were happy to see each other although they had dinner at Michael's only two weeks earlier.

Mary asked 'Where are the boys?'

Maeve said 'Don't look, but they are playing a game and are

hiding from you.' Mary could see a small head behind the couch and walked towards it.

The two boys jumped out saying 'We tricked you Aunty.' It was going to be an enjoyable day.

The boys had been named after members of their families. The older boy was given the names John Patrick Hall and the younger boy Sean Edmund Hall. They would be tall like their father and both had Irish blues eyes like their mother. As usual lunch was a typical country fare. Roast beef and vegetables followed by a 'Rolly Polly' pudding for dessert, and lemonade for the children.

Only general conversation was discussed during lunch although Michael could hardly control himself not to mention his new position and Mary said nothing. After lunch they adjourned to the porch. The women carried their tea and John provided a jug of ale.

John started the conversation and said 'Michael you look very pleased with yourself, is there something we don't know?'

Michael smiled and replied 'Yes as a matter of fact I do, you are now looking at a new Commissioner of Crown Lands.'

John laughed 'Well done and congratulations.' He shook his hand and then clapped, the others did the same.

They were delighted for Michael's achievement. Michael nodded to them and held up his hand acknowledging the applause, they all laughed. He then reminded them of how the appointment originated on the day of his trial and he then told them of the subsequent meetings in Melbourne. He stressed the point that if either Mary or he had a problem with the commitment required by the position, he would resign but both of them thought he should accept the position.

The remainder of the day was an anticlimax after Michael's announcement but they continued chatting, the women about their gardens and the men about their farms.

John walked Michael to the new stock yard fence that he and Connor had erected. The fence was made of iron poles. They would last a lot longer than the wooden poles but they needed to be painted to stop them from rusting. A bull had panicked last week and given the iron poles a good test. John commented that if the fencing had been made of wood he would have smashed through it.

He also showed him the young ram Michael had given him from Elmore. He had matured and was magnificent! He stood proud with his head held high. He would definitely improve John's flock. Perhaps he would produce a Champion or two. Michael and he would be competing against each other at the Kyneton Agriculture Show later in the year. Who would breed the better sheep? Late that afternoon Michael and Maeve headed home.

During the afternoon, Mary had confided to Maeve of the possibility of her being pregnant and the two women conspired to meet in Kyneton and visit the doctor together the following Friday. Mary normally went to town on Friday's for groceries, so the visit would not alert Michael.

Mary had rarely visited a doctor before and was rather apprehensive. The women met at the Botanical Gardens and after a brief chat they shopped for their groceries and then proceeded to Dr Post's surgery.

They had to wait for over an hour and Mary was becoming agitated. Maeve had difficulty trying to ally her fear of seeing a doctor. Finally, 'Mrs. Somerset' was called. The women went in together and were motioned to be seated by a smiling genial middle aged man.

Mary immediately felt comfortable. He asked a few general questions about where was she from and did she know so and so. The questions were designed to establish a rapport between them, and they did. Mary was even laughing at some of their chatter.

Suddenly he asked 'Madam, how can I help you, what is your

concern? Mary was now quietly relaxed, said 'I think I am pregnant.' Dr Post nodded and asked 'Please go behind the screen and we will see.'

Maeve was surprised that Mary stood up and went behind the screen without hesitation. After a few minutes they both returned from behind the screen. Mary was now silent.

The doctor placed both of his hands flat on his desk and said 'Congratulations, you are pregnant Mrs. Somerset.'

Mary's heart was pounding 'Thank you Doctor.'

After so long, it had finally happened. What would Michael say? He had now accepted the position. Maeve put her arms around her and hugged her.

The Doctor continued 'You are healthy but you need to be protective of yourself. Limit your lifting of objects. See me each month so I check your progress. Good day.'

He stood up and opened the door for them and called the next person.

Mary and Maeve drove back to the Botanical Gardens and they sat there for a while looking at the lake with the water hens and wild ducks.

Maeve said 'The doctor is right, be careful what you lift.'

Mary replied 'I can understand that and I will, I want this baby desperately.'

They hugged each other saying 'Goodbye', then stepped up into their gigs and headed to their farms.

Mary started to think of names for the baby when suddenly she remembered what Michael had said, the first born would be named Keogh regardless of the gender. She laughed to herself, thinking well that's one decision already made. She drove the gig to the stable but she couldn't see Dinny, so she unharnessed the horse and put it into the home paddock.

The gig had some groceries in the box and Mary believed that they were not heavy and carried them into the kitchen larder by herself.

Michael rode up from the bottom paddock, with a new born lamb across his knees and saw that the gig was back in the stable. He walked up to the farmhouse carrying the lamb. Its mother would not allow it to feed from her. This was a job with which Mary was familiar. She would patiently feed it from a bottle and hope that the lamb would survive. Most did. The lamb would be kept in one of the stable stalls, for a month or so depending on its being successfully weaned from milk to solid food. Michael started to talk about new lambs being dropped.

Mary waited for him to stop and said 'We need to talk.'

Michael nodded and sat down and waited for her to talk

'I'm having a baby' she said looking at him and then waited for Michael's reaction.

He sat there for a split second then shouted 'Yes! Yes!' stood up and pulled her to him, kissing her gently. He then sat down asking 'When did you find out? When will you have the baby?' He stopped and asked 'Did you know this when I accepted the new job?'

Mary answered honestly. 'I only found out today and if you are worried about my having the baby, it will not affect your position as Commissioner. When my time comes near and if you are away, I will stay with Maeve and John and as Doctor Post lives between both of our farms he is only half an hour away.' Michael sat there thinking that he could not argue with that logic. Even so Michael had mentally decided he would hire a midwife. He would tell Mary later.

Next morning during breakfast, they heard the dogs barking signalling the arrival of a visitor. It was a pleasant surprise, it was John. He jumped from his horse and said 'Congratulations again, a baby and well done Mary.' He paused and then laughed

'And to you Michael of course.' He then handed Mary a bunch of beautiful roses from their garden. John joined them for tea, they talked for a while and then he rode back to his farm.

Michael felt very proud that his wife was pregnant and although he felt protective to her, he knew that she was from farming stock and would be sensible. She would not do anything to put herself, or the child she was carrying, at risk.

Michael now started to think of his position as a Commissioner. He returned to Melbourne court house within the fortnight and after the formality of signing his contract, he was introduced to his fellow Commissioners. They were from different back grounds. Some were like him, experienced farmers and men of note in their communities.

The others had a public service background. He soon realised that the ex-public service Commissioners were lacking knowledge of the Victorian bush culture and were more akin to being too authoritative and/or inflexible and were not experienced at using common sense when dealing with squatters and their land claims. Michael attempted to meet with each of the Commissioners to learn of their methods when handling their responsibilities. Five were helpful but the others were not forth coming. These three were from the public service.

After his induction and training Michael was required to again meet with Magistrate Hogan. His brief advised him of his uniform, but he was surprised at its style. It was a military style uniform in dark green, a few gold braids on the arms and with a blue cap and hessian boots. A pistol holster was also supplied with a revolver and lanyard.

Magistrate Hogan handed Michael his Identity Authorisation and his letter of introduction addressed to the Kyneton Inspector. They shook hands and he wished him the best of good luck. He was required to write a report to him every month detailing his activities. Michael felt self-conscious in his new uniform but he did feel he looked smart. He left Melbourne on a government horse with a government saddle and trappings. He was now a Victorian Government Commissioner of Crown Lands and on his own!

When he arrived back in Kyneton, he stopped at the police barracks to introduce himself. The reaction by the police constables when he entered the foyer was immediate, they all stood to attention. The duty constable immediately went to advise the Inspector. Who came into the room smiling, extending his hand in greeting 'Welcome and please come to my office' he said 'I was not expecting you.'

They sat down and Michael handed over his letter of introduction. The Inspector read it quickly and commented. 'It will be good to have a Commissioner based here. We get several land disputes or queries every month. I'm only new in Kyneton and am feeling my way. Regarding support, I am happy to provide a few constables to assist you on your trips up north. Some of them are in need of bush experience.'

He showed him a small room which he could use as an office. Michael was happy with the meeting but did not stay for long. He was eager to get home.

Michael galloped up the carriageway, and with a flourish pulled up in front of Mary and Dinny, who were feeding the pigs. They both clapped and bowed to the resplendently dressed rider.

Michael dismounted, removed his cap and bowed to Mary saying 'I am your Champion, Madam.' They all laughed.

Michael visited his office each Monday. The second Monday three letters were on his desk. They were all related to land border disputes. One appeared to a simple task but the other two would require his arbitration.

He spoke with the Inspector and it was agreed that Michael would leave Kyneton on the coming Friday with two constables. One was an experienced bush person while the other had been born and bred in Melbourne and had virtually no country experience. They planned to be away for three weeks so they decided to take a small single horse dray and an extra horse.

Mary was quiet but she knew that this is what they had agreed. Friday soon arrived and after a quick kiss farewell, Michael headed to the police barracks to meet up with his team. One of the constables had a cattle dog which it was decided would accompany the team.

The team left before noon and headed north to Heathcote via Redesdale. They estimated to cover fifteen miles a day and would make Heathcote within three days. The ride was uneventful. The constable with the dog drove the dray. The constables would take turns driving.

The first dispute was at the small hamlet of Langley only a few miles from Kyneton. They arrived there mid-afternoon and went to a church behind the inn. The priest lived on the grounds. He complained that a new track had been made by his next door neighbour and it cut across his boundary. Michael checked his complaint and the church records and found that the church had been granted a square covering two acres. The church land had been reduced by the neighbour's track, as the priest had stated. The neighbour had indeed cut across the corner of the church land.

Michael rode to the next door farm and spoke with the farmer, who immediately agreed he was in the wrong and apologised. Michael then supervised a new boundary post being planted. Michael now realised that he had authority which would be accepted almost without question.

Their next stop would be at Axedale north of Heathcote. The

two complainants had been sharing access to a creek, until the farmer up stream had rerouted part of the creek to a new dam due to the dry conditions. Michael knew that water was a life line in the bush and damming a waterway was a very dangerous practice.

The first thing Michael did was to call them together in a room at the local inn. He asked both of them to present their titles. Both titles appeared in order. Michael and his team then visited the creek. Michael was surprised to see so little water in the creek bed. Even above, where the farmer had diverted water to fill his new dam, there was little water flow.

The banks of the creek were over six feet high and there was a mountain range only a few miles further upstream. This creek bed had been a large waterway years ago. With great difficulty they travelled up stream several miles into heavily timbered country, where they found the creek almost blocked by trees and a subsequent soil build up diverting the creek water to a large swamp area where water was consequently stagnant and being wasted.

Michael sent a constable back to town to obtain some explosives. After assessing the blockage by the trees, it was decided it was too dangerous to climb into them and plant the explosives, so they were positioned on top of the largest of the trees blocking the creek and detonated. The explosion blew the top tree apart and copious quantity of water immediately flowed and pushed the remainder of the trees apart and the water went roaring down the creek bed.

When Michael and his team arrived back at the bottom farm, water had filled the creek bed and was flowing strongly. Unfortunately, the farmer sited up stream had his new dam overflow and his farm house suffered some water damage. Michael did not worry about going to see the two farmers. They now both had adequate water for their needs but he doubted if they would ever be friends again He wondered why they had not gone to the trouble of travelling upstream and solving the problem themselves? It was difficult country but the trip would have been worth it.

Michael and his team continued to Wyuna. He had travelled the area before. This was to be a test of his judgement as a Commissioner of Crown Lands. Normally they had camped out in the open. The weather was kind to them, with the days overcast with a little sun and cool evenings. They shot a kangaroo for fresh meat and the older constable made good dampers. They had a water cask on the dray. This was for all, the men, horses and the dog and was topped up whenever they were near water. They were navigating by the sun, a compass and the knowledge of any travellers they met. The area to where they were heading had few roads or tracks and was sparsely inhabited.

They stopped at times to have a chat with the isolated shepherds, boil the billy, or the quart pot as some called it, and use their local knowledge to recheck their course. The shepherd's camps were very basic. Their accommodation was a hut made of a combination of branches, bark, hessian and dried mud. Most seats had three legs due to the uneven mud floor and a table consisting of a large sheet of bark nailed onto the top of some stumps dug into the floor. Empty wooden boxes were the standard cupboards and food bins. They led a quiet and lonely life. Michael would leave, wondering how they mentally handled this way of life.

They rode along rutted tracks and could see dark clouds ahead. Eventually the rains started to pour down. Soon it made the track a quagmire, causing the cart to slide and bounce. At times the driver was nearly thrown from it. They detoured to the grassland. The cart still bounced around but the tussocks were better to drive through than a track with mud filled wheel ruts.

The team eventually reached the settlement of Wyuna, a

sleepy vale nestling in a small stand of trees, on a quiet back water of the Goulburn River. A make shift shack served as the local inn.

A short rotund Irishman ran from the inn to Michael and took hold of his horse's bridle, alternately bowing and doffing his cabbage tree hat. Michael smiled inwardly, his uniform and those of the constables certainly created respect.

The reason Michael was visiting Wyuna was because of an anonymous report, possibly a wandering padre, of the shooting of the local aborigines by a local squatter. An employee of James Knell Esq. a local farmer had been named as the offender.

Led by 'Irish' O'Brien, the team entered the inn and sat at one of the three tables. Bush courtesy prevailed and soon tea and damper were served. Michael indicated he wished to speak with 'Irish' and pointed to the chair opposite him. The innkeeper nervously sat down, with his hands trembling.

Michael said 'I am not here about your license, so you can relax.'

This comment immediately helped to settle the innkeeper nerves. The Irishman smiled and heaved a sigh of relief.

'I am here to investigate the alleged indiscriminate shootings of local aborigines.' Michael paused then continued. 'What do you know of any shootings in this district?'

The Irishman sat quietly and then looked directly at Michael. 'Sir, you must realise that I live here and must not be seen to be implicating any of the locals.' He then stopped waiting for Michael to reply.

'I need you to answer my question. I will not leave here until you do and if you do not give me a reasonable answer you will be arrested by the constables. Do you understand me?' responded Michael firmly.

The Innkeeper quickly answered 'Sir, it is common

knowledge that the overseer at Mr. Knell's property shoots aborigines whenever he wishes, only last week he shot one. There were four aborigines crossing his main grazing paddock and he shot one dead. The other three ran away. His name is Tyne and he is an ex-army private who served in Crimea. I don't think he is right in the head' said Irish.

'Did you see the shooting?' asked Michael.

'No, but I saw the body. He had unusual tribal markings. Each arm had three raised scars above the elbow. The aborigines were not from a local tribe.' he answered.

'What does Mr. Knell do about these shootings?' asked Michael.

'Oh, Mr Knell Sr. lives mostly in Melbourne and I don't think he knows of the shootings. His son came here a few months ago to run the farm.' replied 'Irish'.

Michael asked 'Where is Mr. Knell's property?'

'Irish' went to a window and pulled back a Hessian bag cover and pointed saying 'There it is, Sir.'

Michael followed him to the window and looked out. The main building could be seen between the trees only about a mile away.

Michael decided to call it a day. They would visit the property tomorrow and ask the overseer for an explanation of the allegations levelled at him. After dinner and seeing that the constables were organised for quarters, albeit in the stables, and the horses and dog seen to, Michael retired early to a room provided by the innkeeper.

Morning was heralded by a kookaburra loudly 'laughing' in the distance who was soon joined by several of his feathered friends. The noise was pleasant and very loud but Michael loved this kaleidoscope of sound. He lay on his bunk for a few minutes enjoying the moment. After his normal toiletries, he joined his men for breakfast. The meal was basic but filling, boiled mutton, damper and the ever available tea.

He decided to leave the spare horse and dray together with the dog at the inn. The team fed and watered their horses, then ran their hands over them to check their soundness. One did not want to be out in the bush with an unsound horse. They saddled up, mounted their horses and rode out.

They had left the inn immediately after breakfast and headed down a well-defined track leading to the homestead. They first passed several smaller buildings of rude design. They were typical for the bush, built with slab walls and bark roofs.

As they approached the main house, two dogs ran out barking their greeting. A middle-aged woman walked out onto the veranda and waved. After dismounting and tying up their horses, the team removed their riding gloves and went to meet her. They shook hands and exchanged introductions and she invited them into the house for the customary tea. She also heated some scones and served them with jam, this was a treat for them. The woman explained that she was the house keeper and had only been there for a month.

Michael explained to the housekeeper that he wished to speak to the Overseer, a Mr. Tyne, regarding an incident with an aborigine last week.

The Housekeeper replied 'I can understand why. He is a terrible man, a bully and a drunk. I'm thinking of leaving because of him. I believe that Mr. Knell's son employed him and now he can't control him.' She pointed to a small cabin and said 'He's in there but he'll still be drunk. He was drinking until early this morning. Be careful, he can get nasty.'

Just then a young man walked in and stood looking at them. Michael spoke first and said 'Good Morning I am Commissioner

Michael Somerset.' He stepped forward and they both shook hands.

The other man said 'I'm George Knell, what can I do for you?'

Michael said 'I wish to speak to Mr. Tyne regarding the shooting of an aborigine on your land last week.'

George replied 'I knew that this would happen, he just will not listen. He regards them all as savages. I am at the point of firing him. This has happened before.'

'Did you see the incident of last week?' asked Michael.

'Yes, but regrettably I was too late to intervene. I yelled 'No!' But he still fired and killed the aborigine.'

'Could I rely upon you being a witness for the Crown, regarding this killing?' queried Michael.

George said 'Yes certainly.'

Michael turned to the constables and said 'I think it's time that you arrested Mr. Tyne.' They nodded to Michael and walked over to the cottage

Within seconds of entering Mr. Tyne's hut, shouting could be heard and then a half dressed man was seen to be hurtling through the door and fell sprawling on the ground. The constables wrestled with him and eventually overpowered him and led him to a tree. After they had pulled his arms back behind him and around a small tree trunk, they placed handcuffs on his wrists.

'Were there any other witnesses to the killing?' asked Michael.

George replied 'Two of my shepherds saw him shoot the aborigine. I can take you to them, they are only about two miles away.'

'Good, we can go now,' nodded Michael

Led by George Knell, Michael and the constables rode out leaving a farm hand watching the prisoner who was left safely shackled to the tree.

On reaching the shepherds they all dismounted and sat on large log and started to discuss the killing, when in the distance they heard shouting. Soon they saw the shouting was from the farm hand who galloped up to them. He stopped his horse and breathlessly started talking about three aborigines throwing spears at Mr. Tyne.

The housekeeper was sitting calmly in a rocking chair drinking tea and saying over and over 'I knew he would get his just desserts.'

The riders continued to the tree. They sat on their horses looking down at a bloodied sight. Mr Tyne had three spears in his chest impaling his body to the tree. He was dead. Michael soon overcame the shock of seeing the gruesome sight and asked the farm hand, in which direction did the aborigines go.

He pointed north in the direction of the river. Nothing could be done for Mr. Tyne. Michael nodded to the constables and heading north, they gave chase after the fleeing aborigines.

Michael estimated that the aborigines had about half an hour start on them. They were on good horses, so with any luck they would catch up to them before the river. As Michael rode he pondered. The aborigines must have been watching the homestead and had seen the constables handcuff Mr. Tyne to the tree and took their opportunity to spear him, when the party rode out to speak to the shepherds. At least they didn't harm the farm hand.

The farm hand had pointed to a distant dense tree line running along the banks of the river. It would be difficult to see the aborigines. They were experts at blending into the bush shrubbery. However, Michael's party was obliged to attempt to apprehend them.

The three of them rode apart by a hundred yards. He did not ask the farmer hands for help, he was concerned that they would shoot the aborigines. After a mile or so of riding they settled into a canter. Michael was wondering if they had gone past the aborigines. Were they hiding in the long grass? His question was soon answered. An aborigine appeared from behind a tree a few hundred yards ahead running to the river bank. He ran low and fast between the smaller trees.

The horses and riders were unable to travel fast through the low branches and had to be steered through at a canter. The other two aborigines now appeared running and then separated heading in different directions but generally to the river. They then disappeared as quickly as they had appeared. The river bank was eroded and about ten feet above the water level. As they looked along the river bank, the rider to Michael's left shouted and pointed to the middle of the river.

A bobbing head could be seen swimming with the downstream water flow. The aborigine stayed in the middle of the river and soon vanished around a bend two hundred yards further on. The aborigines had jumped into the river from the high bank. The river was high, flowing fast and turbulent. Next minute one more head rapidly went past Michael's position and vanished around the river bend.

A constable raised his rifle but Michael said 'No.'

They did not see the third aborigine. They waited a half hour then he ordered the constables to head back to the farm for him to complete his report and then to return to the Wyuna inn for a well-earned meal and rest.

At Knell's farm Michael gave the young man a lecture on the responsibility of managing not only the farm but also his employees. A good overseer might be hard to find but he would be better off with no overseer rather than hire a bad one. He also suggested that George advise his father about what had happened and not to let him find out from someone else or worse still, through a newspaper article.

Michael sat outside the inn by himself with a glass of ale thinking of today's event. Inwardly he admired the aborigines' fortitude and tactics. They had run through trees with low branches and had then separated making it difficult for him and his men to apprehend any of them. They had avenged their tribesman's murder and escaped from the white man's law. They would be regarded as brave warriors in their camp tonight. How many other vicious overseers were there out in the bush abusing both aborigines and ex-convict farm hands. The next morning the team headed back to Kyneton.

Mary was now near her time and Michael was being selective with his district visits and the amount of time he spent away from their farm 'Woodlea.' He was now only away for a week at the most and generally addressing local issues. The Magistrate supported this commitment as it was to be only a short term issue. Michael now had a midwife visit Mary daily, she only lived thirty minutes away. Also Maeve visited her every three or four days. It had been decided that Mary would stay with Maeve and John during her last week or so. Michael was happy with this arrangement, although it took a lot of convincing to get Mary to see the wisdom of staying with family and not at her own home.

During Mary's pregnancy, Michael had become adept at handling the different tasks that arose. He had improved the management of many of the grog shanties to an acceptable standard for a wayside inn. Several had lost their licenses and this had made the other licensees realise that the new Commissioner would use his authority without fear or favour.

The ever-present problem of land boundaries had tested his patience several times. Generally he believed that he had resolved most boundary complaints successfully, but he was not naïve enough to imagine that he had been right all the time. He had appeared in court a few times when a decision of his had been overturned by a Magistrate. At times it was a case of who you knew, not if the decision was right or wrong. Michael was not overly concerned as his Superiors supported him in his endeavours. He was handling extremely difficult tasks with a high rate of success and many of the squatters respected him, for his efforts were seen to be fair and reasonable.

The midwife drove Mary to Maeve's farm seven days before their son was born. The baby had arrived several days early.

Consequently Michael arrived two hours after the birth. Mary was well and sitting up holding the new born when he walked into the bedroom.

Michael could not believe a new born baby could be so small. He would not hold the baby as he was worried he might hurt the infant. It would be three weeks before he could be convinced to hold the new born infant. Mary stayed at Maeve's for these three weeks. His family was in good hands and both mother and baby were well.

Michael was happy.

The baby made a difference to their lifestyle. They both had to get used to a baby, demanding to be fed several times a day. Mary enjoyed suckling the baby. Michael also would sit there and watch.

Mary had big breasts and she would tease Michael at times by bouncing them up and down in front of him, after feeding the baby. They both found it difficult dealing with their sleep interruptions. Michael helped as much as he could but it was limited. He soon hired a live-in maid, they could afford it and it did make life much easier for Mary. The maid carried out all the normal domestic duties and she was also good company for Mary.

Michael's next trip was north to the Goulburn River area for a twenty days visit, a week after Keough Seamus Somerset was born. There were a few outstanding problems requiring attention. While he would not admit it to Mary, he was pleased to have a break from his sleep interrupted nights. On their return trip he began to miss his family and became eager to be home again — albeit to more interrupted sleep nights.

The years rolled on. They had a second child, a girl named Maeve-Ann Somerset, in keeping with the inter family names of their son and the Hall's boys. They were all healthy and obviously enjoying country living, 'Woodlea' was prospering and Michael's job as Commissioner was easier and had become almost routine.

The new Land Laws were taking effect. He now carried out most of his work from his office in Kyneton and travelled much less. John, Maeve and their boys were still in close contact. Their two boys were now at school and had grown into fine upstanding young lads. Michael and Maeve still had their strong Irish brogue, and sometimes the boys would copy them in jest.

Both families competed in the annual Kyneton Agriculture Show, attended the Queen's birthday celebrations and local sporting events such as horse racing. Life was predictable and pleasant. The only Kyneton event of major interest for the coming year was to be a planned Royal Tour by His Royal Highness the Duke of Edinburgh who would be visiting Melbourne. The Government wished him to visit a typical Victorian town and Kyneton had been selected. The local Shire Councillors were charged with the responsibility of compiling a guest list of appropriate district identities to be invited to a Gala Ball to be held in His Excellency's honour.

Never had the Councillors been so popular. They were invited to dine in some homes that they would never have seen inside the front door, in the normal course of their council duties. The guest list selection was narrowed down to one hundred couples.

John as the local Ranking Military Officer received an invitation. When his original regiment had been disbanded he had been offered the position of Major of the newly formed Kyneton Mounted Rifles, which he accepted. Michael as the local Commissioner also received an invitation.

They said nothing outside their group as some unpleasantness had arisen from people who had been omitted. The Councillors popularity ebbed and waned with the rumours. Generally the invitation list included successful farmers, business men, senior government officials and community leaders. All in all, the Councillors had creditably performed a very difficult task, as well as could be expected.

The final list was a good cross section of the district citizens. i.e. The local who's who. Gradually, the invitees became known. Some friends were lost, although not for long.

The great day duly arrived. The men's and women's clothes shops had had excellent patronage over the previous two months. Everyone wished to be seen in their best attire, particularly the women. The evening would be more of a fashion show than a formal dinner. Hopefully no two dresses would be the same.

His Excellency travelled by train from Melbourne's Spencer Street station, departing at noon. The journey took Him on a trip through the new suburbs and then into the grasslands north of Melbourne. They passed several small stations where the locals stood and waved small British flags to the delight of the Royal Prince. The train then continued slowly up a long steep incline through the Black Forest area on the west side of Mount Macedon, a few thousand feet above sea level, in the picturesque Macedon Ranges.

Half an hour later the Royal entourage arrived at the Kyneton Railway Station. The station veranda and its buildings had been decked out with red, white and blue bunting. These decorations, together with the local population waving their Union Jack flags, made for a very colourful scene.

The Council visit co-ordinator had arranged for the Mayor and the other Councillors to be assembled as the official welcoming party outside the station platform. When His Excellency alighted from the train there were cheers from the party and the assembled crowd. He waved back graciously.

After a short speech of welcome, the official entourage entered their open four wheel phaeton coaches with matching black horses and proceeded in a parade to their accommodation, after a short diversion via the Botanical Gardens. The early summer blooms were vibrant and showed their colours to great effect. His Excellency acknowledged his admiration of the gardens to the Mayor who was seated opposite Him.

The Kyneton Mounted Rifles had been assigned to provide a Royal Escort. The Riflemen looked immaculate in their red jackets, white breeches and shiny black riding boots and caps. They had been drilling for weeks at local sporting events, to ensure that the horses would not be skittish with the noise from the cheering of the crowds. Major John Hall led the parade with his troop equally divided at the front and to the rear of His Excellency's phaeton.

Behind the rear troopers, came the remaining officials followed by the general public in their gigs and on horseback. Some were even walking. The route streets were lined with cheering citizens together with school children. The pupils had been granted a holiday to celebrate the Royal visit

The parade soon reached the Royal George Hotel where the entire first floor had been booked for the Royal entourage. All of these rooms had been painted and new carpet and furniture provide at the expense of the Council. The Royal Party disembarked from their carriages entered the hotel, giving a quick wave to the crowd who had followed them. They now had a few hours to rest and freshen up prior to attending the Ball, where they were due to arrive at 7 pm.

John returned to the farm to change his uniform. He now wore his Military Dress Uniform with the associated braid and his two medals. He looked almost imperious. Michael dressed in his Commissioner's uniform which in some ways was more resplendent than John's uniform.

The women were more excited than the men about the event. They rarely had the opportunity to dress formally. Maeve and Mary had travelled to Melbourne to purchase their dresses, John and Michael had yet to see them. The four of them agreed to travel together from John's farm. It was a shorter carriage ride into town. Maeve had asked a hairdresser to come to her farm to arrange Mary's and her hair in the latest style that was popular in Melbourne. She arrived at noon and took over two hours to complete her tasks. The time taken was well spent. They were both happy with the result and felt that their hair styles would be the envy of all.

John and Michael were sitting in the lounge room chatting about nothing in particular when the women entered, dressed and ready to be admired.

The men stood up and looked at the women and nodded to each other in appreciation of their wives presentation.

Mary and Maeve laughed, with Mary saying 'We are pleased that we meet with your approval.'

The women were wearing the latest fashion in vogue in Melbourne. Mary was dressed in a royal blue full flowing costume and Maeve in a satin green slim line top and slim line bustle. They had shawls matching their dresses and with their new hair styles, they looked magnificent.

John had invited a photographer to the farm to have a family photograph taken before leaving for the ball. They had been talking about having one done for over year. Now was the time. The children had been dressed by their mothers' several hours ago. The photographer took nearly five minutes positioning them to his satisfaction. The women were seated, the children on the floor sitting sideways, in front of their respective mothers with the men standing behind their wives looking stern. No one was smiling.

The flash from the photographer's equipment was temporarily blinding, but the resultant photograph was excellent. Everyone was happy with the way they were portrayed. However, due to an oversight he could only take the one photograph as he had not brought spare negative slides with him. John was annoyed but it had happened.

The families decided that John should be the custodian and that the photograph would be hung in his library. Mary wrapped the photograph in her shawl. She wished to show it to some friends at the Ball.

It was now time to drive to town. They were required to be seated by 6.30 pm. The children were left in the care of Mary's house maid. The men offered their wives their right arm and escorted them to the coach. They sat quietly in the coach as it clip clopped along the country road in the fresh country air, each happily looking forward to the Ball. Mary still had the photograph in her shawl. She would proudly show it to her friends who would no doubt enviously agree it was an excellent family photograph and to be treasured.

The streets of Kyneton were crowded as never before. John decided to disembark his passengers at the front of the Town Hall and then find a spot to tether the horse and coach. After five minutes, he joined the others in the foyer of the Hall, with invitations at the ready, they walked to the entrance of the main room.

A uniformed usher greeted the Halls and the Somersets. He viewed their invitations, looked up a guest list and advised them that were on table six. Another usher stepped forwarded and indicated that he would escort them to their table. They were delighted to find that they were only two tables from the Royal party. It was exactly 6.30 pm.

They were happily surprised to find that they would be sharing their table with two couples they had known for some time but had not seen them recently. Brendan Devlin was the local Newspaper Editor with his wife Bridget and William Eden was a local businessman with his wife Sarah. Brendan had helped Michael's father during a court case several years ago and William had been instrumental in John buying his farm. The table soon became alive with conversations regarding what had happened since they had last met.

The sound of a bugle fanfare reminded them why they were there. The Royal party had arrived, it was 7 pm. The guests all stood and faced the dance floor. His Highness walked in first, attired in the uniform of a British Regimental Colonel his wife walked slightly behind him as they crossed the dance floor of the ball room.

They were followed by his Aide, the Mayor with his wife and three other members of the Royal Entourage. The National Anthem was played. The Prince sat down, immediately followed by all and sundry. After a moments silence the babble of voices filled the Hall room.

The Mayor rose to the lectern and raised his hand for silence. He then read a prepared speech of welcome to the His Excellency eulogising the importance of His visit to the district and of the loyalty of the Colonists. The speech was short. In succession he proposed a Loyal Toast to the Queen and then a Toast to His Excellency, who then rose to speak. The Prince had a strong voice and responded to the Mayor's speech by acknowledging the patriotic reception he had received during his carriage ride from the Station.

He felt very proud to be here representing his Mother the Queen and that He would advise her of the loyalty of the members of the Colony and in particular, the town of Kyneton. The Mayor then presented the Prince with an embellished scroll on behalf of the citizens of Kyneton, commemorating His visit.

There were no more speeches. John found out at a later date that the Prince had requested a welcome speech only. No doubt he had attended other functions where the speeches had dominated the evening. The Prince wanted this night to be remembered as one of Him meeting the people.

The dinner was served quickly and efficiently. The meals were varied and of a quality which would have surprised even the Royal party. The products were local and fresh as would have been expected from a farming community. There was a multitude of waiters who soon cleared the tables of the empty plates.

The Prince was a man of his word. Immediately after the main course, the Mayor nodded to the band to change their music style from one of background for dining to one for dancing. The Prince and the Princess rose from their chairs as did the Mayor and his wife, when the Royal couple entered the dance floor and commenced a slow waltz, to the applause of the guests. The Prince signalled for other couples to accompany them on the dance floor. Both John and Maeve and Michael and Mary joined the dancers. The dance floor was soon crowded.

Maeve had the surprise of her life when the Prince stopped alongside her and John and requested of John 'Sir. May I have the pleasure of this dance with your wife?' John bowed and stepped back. The Prince and Maeve waltzed away with the Prince talking to her. John bowed to the Princess and stepped forward to dance with her. When the dance was completed He led Maeve back to her table, he had obviously noticed beforehand where she was seated.

When John asked Maeve about what the Prince had said, at first she could not remember. Later she remembered that he had asked her about her life in the Colony as a wife of Military man and a farmer.

The Prince had obviously been briefed by the Mayor about the Hall family. The Prince danced with several women during the evening and He endeared himself to the people with his common touch.

Maeve had handled her moment of fame with aplomb, she had been calm and collected as expected of a Military Officer's wife. John then remembered that his sister had spent quite considerable time with Maeve, teaching her all points of etiquette when she first came over from Ireland to England with John. She had taught her well.

Between dances, the Mayor escorted the Prince to various tables and performed the introductions after giving him a quick brief which allowed easy conversation on an immediate subject with that particular guest.

When they approached table number six, they all stood up the men bowed their heads for a second or two and the women curtseyed, he smiled and nodded to Maeve. The Mayor singled out John and introduced him. The Prince shook his hand and then clasped his hands behind his back, nodding to each of the others.

He commented to John that 'It is pleasing to see that the Colony is now forming their own Military Garrisons with former British Officers as their leaders. Hopefully the recent Maori War has been resolved with benefits to both parties and we can move on together.' He turned to Michael and said 'As a land

Commissioner you must have an interesting Government position. Do you travel a great deal?'

Michael replied 'Generally I'm away for about a week. Yes, it both challenging and rewarding. Our Colony is growing and maturing daily.' The Prince replied 'That is good to hear from a man in your position.' Finally he turned to Brendan, still with his hands behind his back and asked. 'Have you come far for the Ball?' Brendan answered rather abruptly. 'No, I live in the main street.' The Mayor gestured to the Prince, who nodded to all again and walked away with the Mayor, who was briefing him for next table. The Prince had diplomatically not commented on their Irish accent.

When the Prince had departed, John said to nobody in particular. 'I see that the 'Irish' are mellow tonight.' Brendan, Michael and Maeve just smiled and said nothing. If only the Prince had known with whom he had been talking.

Brendan was a through and through Irish rebel and Michael and Maeve had had their moments with the British Authorities in County Clare. Kyneton was long way from their previous troubles. They all now had new lives in a new land — Australia.

At 10 pm the Prince rose from his table, signalling the official end to the Ball. A bugle fanfare sounded.

The guests stood and clapped the official party until they had left the ballroom. The Police provided their escort to the Kyneton station. After more official handshakes, the Royal Entourage boarded the train which then departed for Spencer Station in Melbourne, at 10.30 pm sharp.

They all agreed that the evening had been a resounding success. Kyneton had become the envy of the other Victorian country towns. The Argus newspaper in Melbourne, had had a reporter in attendance and to the delight of the Mayor, he gave a glowing report of the night. He even included a photograph of the table six guests and the Prince speaking with them. When the locals spoke of days gone by, the story of the Prince's visit would always be raised

John and Michael stayed for a few more drinks and gossip. They had agreed to leave at 11 pm. John went to get the coach and bring it to the hall. It would save the women from walking over unpaved streets and soiling the hem of their dresses. Maeve was elected to drive. She turned the horses and headed out of town at a slow trot along the quiet country road.

They were all tired and spoke little on the way home to the farm, actually the men went to sleep. As the night air was getting chilly Mary lent over to get the shawl and when she pulled it towards her the photograph flew out into the night. They halted the coach and looked for it, to no avail.

They came back to the spot next morning but were unable to find it. Sadly, it was the only photograph of the two families ever taken. The occasion for another dual formal family photograph did not arise.

CHAPTER SEVEN

Their Final Journeys

Both John and Michael had resigned from their Government positions and were now 'Men of leisure'. Their farms had been established for many years and were now easy to manage. John and Maeve decided to take the two boys to England to see his family and his family farm. The boys were now grown men. John Jr. was managing the Sunnyside farm for the family while Sean Edmund was learning the wool brokerage business. John Jr had a good overseer, who had taken over from Connor when he retired to live with his relatives in Melbourne. Michael and Mary agreed to keep an eye on the farm and the accounts while they were away.

The Halls were away nearly eight months. The outbound sea voyage was uneventful. . They sailed via Capetown, then direct to Liverpool. John ensured that the John Jr and Sean Edmund did not become too bored. He had them reading British history and Animal Husbandry. He had a discussion session with them daily on these subjects. It helped the time pass.

It was a timely visit as John's father had died during their voyage to England.and his mother survived him by only two months. He had now inherited Brackenshire farm. His sister Maryanne had eventually married William McCarthy who was also a farmer, so she was able to manage Brackenshire farm on John's behalf. He needed time to think of what to do with it. She had her own farm 'Brockelton.' John mused — perhaps Sean Edmund would like to become a farmer, albeit in England. The father and the son had a long discussion over the matter. Sean liked the idea of following in his father and grandfather's footsteps. He decided to stay in Cumberland for the time being and see if he wanted to be an English farmer and also if he was capable of managing Brackenshire. Mary-anne and William would take him under their wings. After a month, John and Maeve returned home. John had felt the loss of his father very badly but he had wanted to return home to Victoria.

Sadly six months after returning, John endured the sadness of Maeve's death from Typhoid. John felt the loneliness that grief brings. He was thankful that John Jr. was with him at the farm. He kept himself occupied by helping with the management of the day to day farm tasks and keeping the account books. Michael and Mary still visited every two weeks or so. John drove the gig to Kyneton each week to have lunch and an ale with a group of friends from his Military days. He eventually decided to write his auto biography. This became a start/stop task that would keep him occupied for several years.

After John's family had returned to Victoria, Mary suggested to Michael that they take a trip to Ireland. The political scene had changed for the better. Although it still had a long way to go to be acceptable to the Irish population.

Michael had become a very wealthy man so the cost of the trip was of little concern to him. He agreed, with the children cheering at the thought of them travelling to another country.

John said he would keep an eye on their farm 'Woodlea.' Dinny had retired but he still pottered around the farm doing odd jobs. He still lived on the farm and was provided with food and a small stipend, because of his good and faithful service to the Somersets. Michael had him built a small three roomed dwelling behind the shearing shed, which Dinny shared with the new farm hand, who he had recommended as his replacement. Michael advised John that if Dinny said that he needed to

hire a casual, just let him do it and bill his account and to keep
an eye on Tabu to see if he was well.

Over the years, Michael had kept in touch with Tabu and
used him to help out from time to time. The Yandarbee tribe still
lived in the Black Hills only half an hour's ride from Woodlea
farm. Michael still did some short term droving and took Tabu
and his son Jimmy, with him. He normally only needed one
stock hand. Tabu had brought his son to show Michael, when
the boy was sixteen years old and now they would always arrive
just when Michael was preparing to go droving or shearing. No
doubt the 'Bush telegraph' was active. Jimmy was a good worker
and trustworthy. Michael now had five hundred acres and running several hundred sheep, and was teaching Jimmy to shear.
Tabu was still helpful around the shearing shed and the farm in
general. Michael had a few milking cows, some pigs and several
horses and he had built several horse stalls down by the river.

Over the years, Tabu's tribe had dwindled to only twelve.
Most families had moved further north with the increase of
the farms encroaching onto their hunting lands. The younger
aborigines were working on the farms and in town as labourers. The rapid growth of the Colony had not been kind to the
aborigines. The aborigines without jobs migrated to towns and
had become a nuisance with their begging. Unfortunately, they
were treated with contempt.

Michael sat on the veranda reading the paper. The headlines were — Bushrangers in the Black Forest. He put the paper
down, the headlines reminded him of an incident he and Tabu
had several years ago, when they were 'Bailed up' by bushrangers. At the time it wasn't funny but later Michael often had a
quiet chuckle about what had happened.

Tabu and he had been shearing at a property near Tooborac
a day or so ride from Kyneton. They had shorn three hundred

sheep and had been paid with gold sovereigns. He put them in a small leather bag and placed them in the seat box of the dray. Early morning, he and Tabu set off for Kyneton on a long curving road. The scenery in this district was one of green bush, tall trees and a myriad of colourful birds. The area was famous for its gigantic volcanic boulders on the surrounding hills. The day was cold and Tabu had his possum skin cloak wrapped him.

At noon they had stopped to eat and water the horse at the top of a hill. As they were about to leave, Tabu walked to centre of the road and pointed 'Horse he go long der little time.'

Michael immediately thought of Bushrangers. There were no recent sheep or cattle hoof marks or dung on the track only horse shoe prints. Tabu climbed a tree and pointed down the road ahead of them.

When he climbed down he said 'Men sit little way down der.'

Michael thought for second and then said. 'Put your trousers in the seat box.'

He then handed the bag of sovereigns to Tabu saying 'Put this in your possum skin and follow me alongside of the road, but stay hidden in the bush.' Michael continued 'If they stop and want to rob me, when I put my hands up in the air, make noises like many aborigines. Do you understand me?'

Tabu nodded. 'Make plenty noise like fight.' Michael nodded.

Tabu vanished in the bush, as Michael drove the dray down the track towards where he thought the possible bushrangers were. Within ten minutes, he came around a bend and three mounted riders were lined across the road. One had a pistol and another had a shotgun. The third rider was an unarmed young boy.

The one with the pistol said. 'We will cause you no harm, just step down and give us your watch and your money.'

Michael stepped down and nervously answered, 'I have no watch and only a little money.'

The man with the shotgun walked over to Michael and said menacingly 'Empty your pockets.'

Michael extracted a sovereign and two florins and gave them to him.

The man with the pistol then said to the youth 'Search the dray and see what he has in it.'

The youth did as he was told. He found Michael's shot gun and shearing gear and some old clothes. He held them up for the other two to see.

The first man said 'You seem to be as poor as we are. We will take your shot gun and also your belt.'

The man had noticed that Michael was wearing a military belt that John had given him. The man with the shotgun started swearing and approached Michael pointing his gun at him. Michael raised his hands into air.

Immediately Tabu started yelling and screaming, darting between bushes, making it appear that there were several natives. The bushrangers looked towards the noise and saw Tabu, semi naked, waving at them.

The bushrangers yelled 'Aborigines, let's get out of here or we'll all be killed.' and ran to their horses and swiftly rode away towards Kyneton, taking Michael's shot gun and belt with them.

Tabu walked back to the dray handed the money bag to Michael and said. 'Dey hab horse wid funny foot.' He pointed to the ground. One horse had a shoe that was bent.

As they drove towards Kyneton they stopped every half hour or so. Each time they stopped, they were able to identify the bent horse shoe. The Bushrangers were heading for Kyneton. Michael decided to continue to Kyneton without stopping and they arrived early evening. He immediately went to the Police Barracks and reported the robbery.

The sergeant said 'You are the third report we have had this week.' Michael then explained that his farmhand had tracked the unusual horseshoe into Kyneton.

It was decided that at daybreak the Police, with Tabu leading, would check every stable in the main street and then the side streets. Tabu almost ran up and down the main street looking for an imprint of the bent horse shoe. After an hour with no success they started to check the side streets. At the third street an imprint was found that led to a small house.

The Police decided to wait a while, as they knew that the Bushrangers were armed and the Police wished to avoid a gun fight so close to the main street.

About noon, the young boy who had been with the Bush-rangers, walked out the front door and entered the stable at the side of house. A short time later he reappeared leading a horse and headed to the water trough around the corner in the main street. The Police did not follow him, as they were seeking the two adults.

Michael, who was waiting in the main street, saw the boy when he left the shack. He waited until the horse was drink-ing and the boy distracted. He then walked up behind him and grabbed him. The boy was shocked but did not struggle. Michael could see that he was young, no more than fourteen years of age.

He told him 'Don't go back to the house or you will be caught and go to gaol.'

He then said to the boy. 'I'll give you a chance to grow up and not be a criminal, if you get on your horse, get out of Kyneton and don't come back.'

The boy was shaking but he nodded, mounted his horse and quickly rode down the street and vanished into the hills. Michael felt good. He would have felt uncomfortable being involved in the gaoling of a person so young. But he had no sympathy for the two grown bushrangers.

The Police waited until the two men left the house and then surrounded them with their pistols drawn.

They surrendered saying 'What have we done?'

Even when they saw Michael, they continued to plead ignorance. The house was searched and among the articles found inside were Michael's shotgun and military belt. At the police station, they were shown the shot gun and belt. They said that they owned them.

The Police Sergeant looked at Michael and asked him. 'Can prove that these items are yours?'

Michael stepped forward and turned the belt over and inside was a brand in the shape of a key.

'Yes, that is my brand,' he replied.

He went to the shot gun and removed the front grip, inside was the same brand. The Police Inspector had walked in unnoticed and was standing behind them all and was listening.

He then walked forward looked at the brand and said 'That is Mr. Somerset's brand.'

He then turned nodded to Michael and said 'Good morning Mr. Somerset.'

One bushranger turned to the other and said to the other 'You thought he was poor.'

The sergeant walked over to Michael and said 'I thought you said that there were three of them.'

Michael said 'No, I was mistaken.'

He looked at the bushrangers and they both slightly nodded to him — a silent thank you for not mentioning the young boy.

Following their arrest, bushranger activities in the district ceased abruptly. The penalty for the two offenders was 10 years in gaol. Unfortunately this sentence did not deter others from following in their footsteps. Tabu's role in the apprehension of the bushrangers gained him some notoriety. He was in demand as a black tracker by the authorities but he preferred his life the way it was.

A month prior to Michael departing for overseas, Tabu arrived at the farm. He was by himself.

Michael took him to the barn and sat with him. 'What's wrong Tabu?' asked Michael.

Tabu said 'Lubra die, Jimmy he go wok long Gulbin Riber. Me want live long farm longum yu riber house and wok farm.'

Michael thought for a moment then he realised that Tabu wanted to live in a horse stall on the river bank. There was no doubt that it would be much better than living under a bark mia mia in all weathers. After all he and Tabu had done together, how could he not help him?

Michael nodded in agreement. 'I will give you clothes and food and some money and you can help around the farm. But only you come, no more Yandarbee man.'

Michael didn't want to have an aboriginal camp on his farm, particularly when he would be away for several months.

Tabu nodded and said 'No boss, Tabu tasal.'

Tabu stood up, picked up his few possessions, walked to the river bank and sat down. Tabu had aged, his time was coming. He would be happy sitting on the bank of the Campaspe River gazing into its cool, clear babbling waters. Michael found out later that the tribe had totally disbanded when timber cutters had started working in the Blackhills. He never did find out what happened to the tribe's older people.

Michael took the coach to Melbourne to arrange their sea passage. He located a ship sailing via Rio De Janiero and then to Cork. With the predominately westerly winds it would be a faster voyage than going via Capetown. He would book their return voyage when they decided it was time to return home.

The departure day arrived and they started their journey

with a gig ride to the Kyneton Station, then a train ride to Spencer St and finally a hansom cab to the pier. The ship was aptly named the SS Discovery, it was a large three mast sailing ship. They had a large cabin with four bunks. There was little privacy but it was comfortable, it was on the main deck and had two port holes. As first class passengers, they were greeted by Captain James Steele, a veteran Yorkshire sailor. A sailor carried their luggage to their cabin and showed them the amenities, such as they were on a sailing ship. There were only two other couples on board, and a Military officer travelling in first class with ten solders under his command, in steerage class.

The soldiers were returning to England after completing five years service in the Colony of Tasmania (the former Colony of Van Diemen's Land). The ship was delivering Tasmanian pine to Rio De Janiero and then collecting a cargo of sugar cane for several Irish Merchants in Cork.

The ship cast off on the morning's low tide to ensure that they would reach the Port Phillip Bay Heads late afternoon on an outgoing high tide. The heads was notorious for its turbulent rush of water exiting the bay from a high tide.

If the Captain timed the ship's exit from the bay with the water out flow correctly, the sea might be a little rough but it would flow out in a straight line carrying the ship with it and safely clear the rocks either side of the bay's watercourse.

The Somerset family stood outside their cabin and watched Melbourne's Hobson Bay disappear in the north. The sails were full, with the north westerly wind blowing at about ten knots. They sailed to the east of the bay heading towards Sorrento, then turned to the south west to line up with the Heads. The ship picked up speed and then, with a rush, the ship sailed between the Heads out into waters of Bass Straight. It had taken a half an hour of good seamanship and knowledge of the area to make a potentially difficult task look easy. Many ships had been sunk in this area.

The Captain now plotted his course to the east, avoiding the islands in Bass Strait, again with the north westerly filling his sails. Soon the wind would be from the west with ship heading for the tip of the south coast of South America.

Michael had taken a tip from John and had brought items along to keep Keogh and Maeve-Ann occupied. He had selected Animal Husbandry for Keogh. Michael secretly hoped Keogh would become a farmer, although Keogh had almost completed three years at the Melbourne University studying Engineering and Science. He had also brought some of his study books.

Mary had selected Tapestry and Crochet patterns, with the necessary instructions, needles and cottons etc. Both mother and daughter enjoyed needlework and had completed some excellent doilies, table settings and wall hangings. Michael intended to read whatever he could get his hands on.

Michael sat on a bollard on the deck by himself and reflected on his ship's voyage as a convict. This was in total contrast — from the bilges to first class. He laughed quietly to himself. Perhaps the British Government had done him a favour. If he hadn't been sentenced he might still be an Irish tenant farmer or worse.

When they reached Cork he intended to locate Patrick, his brother with whom he had lost contact. Then meet with his cousin James Keogh in Kilrush, perhaps Uncle Jack and Aunt Anne too, if they were still alive? Finally he would visit his father's and Aunt Jane and Uncle Sean Keogh's farms. It had been nearly forty years since he had left County Clare. Would they recognise him or had his uncles and aunties had passed on?

What would the town and the farms look like? Michael had so much anticipation. He hoped he wouldn't be disappointed. Mary had no such expectations.

She had no family other than Michael and their two children and she was content if they were all happy. She sat and watched Maeve-Ann needling away, humming to herself. Their daughter was a very happy young woman. Keogh would read for a few hours then go out on deck and talk with the young Midshipmen. Most of them were younger than he was. He asked questions and listened intently to their answers.

He had even borrowed some books from them on navigation. At one stage he said to his father casually. 'I wonder what it would be like to be a Navy Officer?' Michael thought no more about Keogh's comment.

They socialised with the two couples and the Military Officer. Playing cards and chatting over afternoon tea. They were a compatible group and enthusiastic about the Colony's future. Michael had read most of the books on board the ship. He swapped them with the other passengers. The voyage to South America had been uneventful. Land appeared in the distance. Coincidently at the same time the sea swell increased and the wave tops became white with spray from the wind.

At the Captain's table that evening, he advised them that the trip around the tip of South America was generally with high and uncomfortable seas and that the passengers should remain in their cabins until instructed otherwise. Michael had already stowed and tied down their luggage to avoid any possible injury to them. They could see Terra Del Fuego (The land of lights) through their port holes. They were now sailing in the seas flowing between the southern islands of South America and the mainland. The heavy seas continued for nearly two days and made everyone miserable. At times sailors brought them meals but little was eaten.

Fortunately the Somerset's cabin was in the middle of the ship so they felt the pitching and rolling less than some of the other passengers in steerage. Although they felt nauseous at times neither of them was sea sick. Finally the seas abated, when the ship turned into the Atlantic Ocean and calmer waters, as they heading northward. During a chat with the Captain next day, he commented to Michael, that the seas had been less rough than at other times. Previously he had had injured passengers and sailors and had lost rigging. He said several of the solders had been sea sick but there were no injuries this time.

Rio De Janiero looked spectacular with its long white beaches and Mt Sugarloaf overlooking the city. The ship only stayed for twenty six hours. The unloading, loading and collecting food, water and some live stock had taken less than a day. Captain wanted to use the same tides in and out of the harbour. Michael took the family ashore to stretch their legs and to do a little sightseeing. They hired a small coach and driver and spent five hours being shown around the scenic views of the city and the harbour. They all agreed it had been worth the effort.

As they sailed further north they could feel the change in the air temperature. They had left Melbourne in April and it was now July. They would arrive in Ireland in summer which was the best time to visit the northern hemisphere.

The youngsters would not have appreciated a northern winter. Even the summer temperatures would be cooler than what they had been used to.

A week before arriving in Cork, the Captain provided a special meal for his first class passengers and his officers. He had been saving the best until last. Prior to this meal, the repast had been rather ordinary. Poultry purchased in Rio had been prepared with fish and fresh vegetables and had been followed up with fresh fruit and honey. Port and cigars were offered to the men while the women were offered a sherry. The youngsters had lemonade.

The Captain made a short but eloquent speech, which he had probably used many times previously. He then presented each male passenger with a small scrimshaw engraved with a model of his ship, and the women with an embroidered handkerchief with the ship as an embroidered feature. The select guests applauded the Captain acknowledging the excellent meal and their presents. It had been a pleasant evening.

Ireland appeared off the starboard bow. Michael had tears in his eyes. His family stood by his side and enjoyed looking at the coast of Ireland for their first time. The hills were delightfully green and contrasted magnificently with the blueness of the sea. As they sailed closer to the shoreline, the buildings became more distinct. Small white cottages and out building were dotted over the hillsides. Years ago these were sparse, on almost vacant lands. Yes, Michael could expect vast changes in the landscape from when he lived here as a boy.

The ship had most sails furled as it slowly sailed up the River Lee. Two large row boats came along side. The ship furled its last sails and ropes were thrown to the row boats. Then the two boats manoeuvred the SS Discovery to a pier where dock hands moored the ship to the pier bollards. They had arrived in Cork.

After the ships walkway was lowered, several port officials immediately came aboard as Michael and his family was preparing to leave the ship. One group spoke with the Captain. The second group visited the passengers. They knocked on Michael's cabin and were invited to enter. They asked a few basic questions. Who are you? Where are you from? Why are you here? How long are you staying? They all possessed Colonial identification papers. Michael showed them the papers and said that they were visiting relatives and would be here around three months.

A quick 'Thank you Sir' and the officials left the cabin.

Several small four wheel horse coaches were at the bottom

of the walkway waiting for fares. Michael approached the first in line and asked for hotel accommodation?

The driver said 'Yes, the Shamrock Hotel would suit you Sir.'

Michael returned aboard and asked a sailor to bring down their luggage.

The Captain approached him saying. 'I enjoyed having you and your family aboard. I trust that we will meet again.'

They shook hands and went their separate ways. The family boarded the coach and the driver headed the horse into town, pointing out sights of interest.

The Shamrock Hotel was a European designed building over-looking the river. Nothing had been spared in its construction to bring it to its current state of opulence. The driver carried their luggage into the foyer and left pleased with the tip Michael had given him.

They selected a three bedroom suite on the top floor. They each commented it was good to have some space and privacy again. After unpacking, they each had a long hot bath and spent the rest of the day relaxing. The housemaid had not been impressed at having to draw four lots of bath water. They had an early dinner and soon retired to bed. Tomorrow would be the start of their visit.

Michael rose early and visited several shipping agencies enquiring after Patrick. He left notes with these agents, hoping to meet up with Patrick prior to leaving for Kilrush. He did not expect to have any luck finding him but he felt that he had to try. After two hours and no luck he returned to the Shamrock Hotel.

The others were all dressed and waiting. Over breakfast he told them where he had been and they understood. They decided to stay in Cork for a few days and explore the area. They hired a small four wheel coach and driver who showed them around the district. The youngsters had not realised that there had been so many Castles from times gone by. Most were now derelict and only of interest to visitors. They took a boat trip up stream, visited the cathedrals, marvelled at the size of the harbour and the number of ships moored. However three days was enough. Michael was more interested in locating his remaining family members — if any were still alive? Next morning he found a coach agent and booked the family to go to Kilrush, his birth place, the following day. They had enjoyed staying at the Hotel. It would be a while before Melbourne would have first class hotels such as the Shamrock Hotel.

Next morning they were up and away to Kilrush. Michael remembered it as a small town with a harbour sited on the mouth of the Shannon River. But that was a long time ago. After several team changes with fresh horses and short meal breaks, they were off again.

They shared the coach with two other people, who identified themselves as Kilrush locals. Michael asked if they knew of any Keogh residents in that district.

The older man nodded and said 'Yes, there is a family in the township with that name but I don't know where they live. They have a family shipyard on the docks.' Michael's heart missed a beat. He immediately thought Uncle Jack, Aunty Anne and Cousin James. It had to be them.

Michael's heart was racing with excitement. Mary sensed his mood and squeezed his hand. The children were unaware of the impact of the answer their father had received.

The coach came to the top of a hill which overlooked the harbour town. Michael could not believe his eyes. The town was now a small city with buildings as far as he could see. The horses cantered on down past some buildings Michael recognised.

The old Army Barracks, the Constabulary offices, the Custom Building and the infamous work house, that housed the poor during the famine, were still there but now had different uses. Memories came flooding back. He sat back in his seat not saying a word. Mary left him to his thoughts.

The coach stopped in front of the Kilrush Arms Hotel, while the other passengers were alighting, Michael went into the Hotel enquiring about accommodation availability. Receiving an affirmative answer, Michael signalled the coachman to lower their luggage from the coach top. Mary, Keogh and Maeve-Ann had alighted and entered the Hotel, while Michael found a baggage porter.

They were given three rooms together on the top floor facing the pier. Keogh sat at his window for a while, enjoying the view of the ships on the river. The Hotel was clean and comfortable but not as luxurious at the Shamrock in Cork. Again they had an early dinner and retired early.

They arranged to meet for breakfast at 8 am. While dining, Michael asked each of them what they wanted to do. Mary and Maeve-Ann said they would like to look around the town, albeit, the shops. Keogh shrugged his shoulders and looked at his father enquiringly.

Michael said. 'Right, away you two go, Keogh and I will be going to the ship builder's district at the docks and hopefully we will locate my Cousin's business.'

Michael followed his father out of the Hotel and they walked to the docks about a mile away. They strolled along looking at the moored vessels. Some were Man of War ships flying the Union Jack. The most impressive ship was the HMS Arrow with its large compliment of guns and tall four masts. They reached the entrance to the docks and were challenged by an old salt in a battered uniform.

Who asked in a deep voice 'What might your business be, Sur?'

Michael replied 'I'm here to visit my cousin, James Keogh at his ship yard.'

'Aye, you'd be in luck Sur. He being just arrived ten minutes ago.' The old salt tipped his cap to them then stepped back allowing them to pass. Michael became excited, the coach passenger was right. The Keogh's shipyard was still operating.

Would they recognise each other after all of these years? The shipyard was bigger than he remembered but he still recognised some buildings from when he served here as a young apprentice. He stood outside the office door looking into the boat shed.

A voice asked. 'Good morning, what can I do for you?'

He turned a saw a solidly built man who he knew was Jack Keogh's son. It was James.

Michael said 'I would be surprised if you knew who I was, but I recognise you — James Keogh.'

James looked curiously at Michael and said. 'I feel I should know you, but!'

Michael said 'I am Michael Keogh your cousin from long ago.'

James was silent for a second and then said 'No, I can't believe it after all of these years. Come in! Come in!' He repeated excitedly and motioned them to be seated

Michael interrupted 'This is my son Keogh.' James looked puzzled at the name as they shook hands.

Michael laughed 'I'll explain it later.'

They both started to talk at once. James put up his hand and said. 'This reunion will take some time to discuss. Can I suggest that we meet tonight? I unfortunately have a boat to hand over today and I'm a day late. But I am free for the next few days.'

Michael asked. 'Can we meet tonight at the Kilrush Arms for dinner? I have my wife and daughter with me also.'

'Yes. I am also married with a son, we'll all come. Can we agree 7 pm?'

Michael nodded. There was a knock on the office door. It was James's Boatswain, he was ready to sail.

James stood up and said. 'I'm very sorry but I must go, we'll meet at 7 pm.'

Michael sat there for a moment. He had found James! Keogh looked at him and stood up waiting for his father to join him. They walked back to the Hotel with Michael telling Keogh of his youthful days in Kilrush.

Michael told Mary of their meeting with James and that they had arranged for the two families to meet for dinner that night. Mary began to fuss over each of them. She wanted the Somerset's to create a good first impression with their recently found family relatives. Michael laughed, he enjoyed her when she became bossy.

They were seated in the hotel dining room, when Keogh nodded to his father. Michael turned his head to see James walking towards them accompanied by a lady and a lad around Keogh's age. They all stood Michael introduced his family first and then James introduced his wife, Bridget, a red haired west coast Irish woman and then his son, Jack, presumably named after his grandfather. They sat opposite each other so that the men could converse directly, the women and then the youngsters sat likewise.

Michael started the conversation first by enquiring of James parents. He was not surprised when James said that they had passed on over five years ago. They both had been seventy-five years of age. James had worked with his father since leaving school and when his father died he decided to remain in the shipyard business. He now employed ten shipwrights and fourteen labours. It was a profitable business and he was well respected in the County. Michael noticed that Keogh was listening intently and asked a few questions about what size were their ships and where did they sail. Seeing Keogh's interest, James invited him to spend a day with him and Jack at the shipyard.

Michael then explained the reason that he was now named Somerset. James family was enthralled to hear Michael's extraordinary story in the Colonies. Meals were served during his discourse. He started with his imprisonment at Port Arthur and spoke for over ten minutes, finishing with their farm at Kyneton.

James sat there shaking his head and said 'If someone else had told me your story I would not have believed them. You have had an extraordinary adventurous life.'

Jack asked about the animals in Victoria. Keogh then spoke up and described some of them, the kangaroo, platypus and the wombat. The two boys warmed to each other. Mary and Bridget were somewhat reserved at first but eventually they found common ground discussing needlework and the differences in their social activities. Maeve-Ann sat there quietly listening and only spoke when answering a question. The evening was drawing to a close. James invited them to join his family for dinner in two days' time, at his home. James would send a coach for them. They all rose and bid each other goodnight. The evening had been most enjoyable for all.

The next morning the Somerset's walked to Michael's old school. It was still there but several rooms had been added. It was now more obvious and the building no longer hidden from the road by large bushes, as it had been in the bad days of the 1840 and 50's when the British discouraged educating the Irish Catholics. The church was still the same size but was in an extreme stage of disrepair. The weather boards on the walls were badly cracked with the paint peeling, and the grounds were over grown with weeds and long grass. He found out later that the local priest had died several months ago and the parish was still waiting for a replacement. Obviously the parish needed a leader.

They walked back to the main street where Mary took charge and walked them through the market and shops. Maeve-Ann bought a souvenir doll dressed in an Irish tartan. Michael couldn't remember what his tartan was?

Most of the day was spent wandering around Kilrush streets and lanes. Many of the old buildings were still in good condition with several new Government office blocks complimenting the town.

The town was generally neat and tidy, even with all the animal traffic transiting the main street. The remainder of the day was spent with them just idling around the hotel reading or chatting with the locals in the bar.

Michael tried to delay visiting his father's old farm until he had a chance to speak with James, but he could not resist the urge to go next day. He rose early, leaving a note that he would be back around noon. He hired a gig and headed north out of town. He trotted passed several sites that he remembered. He recalled seeing them have their hovels torn down. They now had small houses built on them. County Clare had changed for the better. As he rounded a bend he looked to the right to see the place where he had been involved with the constable's horse which ultimately caused him to be transported to Van Diemen's Land. Memories came flooding back.

Another hour saw him at the road down to his father's farm.

Tentatively he drove to the farm entrance. The farm was being worked. He could see vegetable beds, fruit trees and several sheep. There was no horse or dray around and there was no smoke coming from the chimney. He turned the gig around and then headed to where Aunt Jane's farm was. There was the same situation. Both farms were being worked but no one was around. He sat there for a while and then decided he would return tomorrow. He headed back to town, arriving just in time for lunch with family.

The following morning, Bridget and Jack arrived at the hotel in a small coach. Bridget offered to take Mary and Maeve-Ann to a social gathering and drop Jack and Keogh at the shipyard. They gratefully accepted her invitation. Michael had already left to visit the farms again.

Mary and Maeve-Ann observed Bridget's dress style and dressed accordingly. She advised that they were going to attend a school fete. The fete consisted of speeches, tea and scones and an auction of donations of craft ware — paintings, embroideries etc. with the proceeds going to the church maintenance fund.

Bridget was well known and had many friends. Mary and Maeve met many of them but they had trouble remembering their names. Being from the Colonies they were regarded with interest and were in demand for a chat.

Jack and Keogh were compatible and spoke freely with each other. James asked Jack to walk Keogh through the shipyard and explain the procedure to build a boat, starting with — the contract — the basic design — the plans — the materials — the jigs needed — the work skills needed — the manufacture of the frames etc — the assembly — the detailing of the boat and finally the sea trials. Keogh found the day's experience very interesting and asked many questions, which delighted Jack by allowing him to show his knowledge.

Michael repeated yesterday's activity. He hired a gig and retraced his trip to the farms. This time as he entered the first farm he could see smoke coming from the chimney. A dog ran out barking. And it was soon followed by a tall man about sixty years of age. Who was he? As he got closer — No it couldn't be

— Patrick? Michael left the gig and walked towards him. The man looked closely at him and, said with astonishment 'Is that you Michael?'

Michael nodded then said 'Patrick.' and then put his arms around him. He had tears in his eyes. They walked in silence into the farm house.

Patrick said 'I had given up the hope of ever seeing you again.'

Michael answered 'Maeve wrote several times to Aunt Jane but received no answer. We presumed that she had died and we knew that Uncle Sean was not interested in writing. So she stopped writing several years ago. She wrote to you in Cork but we received no reply.'

'Yes, I went to Dublin soon after you left. Aunt Jane had my address. But she stopped writing to me also. I found out later that she had gone blind so I came back to run the farms. Sean wasn't interested. He's still alive and lives in town in a home for Seafarers.' Michael looked at him waiting for him to continue. 'Yes, Aunt Jane died several years ago. She asked me to run the farms and keep them in the family.

I live in this one but I visit the other farm house nearly every day and work the vacant third farm land.'

Michael said 'Good, are they making money?'

Patrick replied 'Yes, not a lot but I have money in the bank and I give money to Sean when he asks.' He paused 'Incidentally you need to know what has happened over the years, regarding land ownership. After the Corn Laws were abolished, Ireland became a somewhat better place to live. The British Government changed some of their land controls over Ireland. They moved most of their administrators out of Clare and allowed us locals to assume some responsibility for our destiny, including the farm lands. From this change, some complaints arose regarding land ownership decisions.'

He continued. 'When the new officials investigated the applications, they were unable to find official claims for many of the small holdings. A decision was made that — Tenants who could prove more than two generations of occupancy by the same family would have first choice of claiming ownership.'

'No one applied for our properties, so I applied for ownership of these two properties and the third one which had been vacant since 1845 when our uncle went to America and vanished. With letters of support from Uncle Jack, your school friend Barry Daniher who is a well-known coastal Sea Captain and Jamie Neyland the well-known patriot, I was interviewed and was able to prove at least three generations and lo and behold, I became the legal owner of the three farmlands on two titles. If I had known that you were alive or your whereabouts, I would have put your name and Maeve's on the titles.'

Michael put his hand up, stopping him and said sadly 'I'm sorry to have to tell you, Maeve died last year and you have probably guessed that our father has also passed on. He fell from a gig several years ago and died from the fall.' Patrick sat there quietly with tears in his eyes.

Michael continued 'We had a typhoid epidemic and she unfortunately contracted it.' After a moment or two Michael said 'I already have a good farm. The titles to these farms are yours alone.'

Michael and Patrick sat talking until late afternoon. Michael said he would return tomorrow with his family. It was getting dark when Michael arrived back at the hotel. The family had dinner while discussing what they had done during the day. They had each enjoyed their day.

After dinner Michael went to the bar and sat by himself, thinking of today's meeting with his brother, who he had not seen for over forty years. He was delighted that the ownership of the land had now being legalised. It had been a problem for his forefathers for many, many years.

Michael advised his family that they were going to the family farms in the morning. They had an early breakfast and he then went and hired a four wheel coach and returned to the hotel to find the family waiting in the foyer. Michael acted as tour guide on the way to the farms.

The family sat quietly just listening and looking, the sun was pleasant as was the view of the rock walls separating the rolling green pastures. The horse trotted along with the coach bouncing gently from side to side. The land appeared to be greener than Victoria's. He pointed out where the house had been when he grabbed the constable's horse's reins and how he had eventually been arrested.

They went to Patrick's home farm first and Michael proudly introduced his family to him. His farm house had another room added and much improved furniture. A cupboard showed off the crockery and there were side tables with ornaments. The floor was now made of wood, covered by some small carpets. Patrick then took them on the short walk to the Cliffs of Mohr, to show them the view of the Atlantic Ocean and the sheer cliff face with myriads of birds nesting in the crevices. A walk through the vegetable garden, which impressed Mary, and then up to Aunt Jane's farm house completed the walk. The farm house windows were still covered in lace curtains, dusty but still showing quality. The crockery was in the cupboards made by Michael, from the shipyard off cuts, many years ago. The Bedrooms were clean but dusty. The beds and the furniture had been covered with calico covers since Aunt Jane's death.

Again this farm had another vegetable garden. Patrick was grazing sheep on two of the farms, while on the third farm he had sown corn and wheat. The crops were very healthy. He was a good farmer. The scene was completed with two horses and a two wheel dray.

Mary commented on the view from Aunt Jane's farm house.

Patrick said immediately 'Why don't you stay here for a while and enjoy the Irish country air?'

Keogh seized on the moment, looked at father and asked 'Can I stay with James then? I like going to the shipyard.'

Mary looked at Maeve-Ann who nodded and agreed 'I like it here. Mother and I can help with the vegetables and go for walks with the dog.'

Michael turned to Patrick and said 'Well it looks like you will have neighbours for a while. We have no set date to return home. We'll probably be here for a month or so'

It was agreed that they would now return to town to arrange their move and return to the farm the next day. On the way back to the hotel, Michael went via the shipyard to ask James if Keogh could stay with them for a while. Both James and Jack thought it was a good idea and said that he was welcome to stay as long as he liked. Everybody was happy.

The next day James and Jack stopped at the hotel to collect Keogh and his baggage. He waved happily to them, as he left for the shipyard. Michael had arranged for a coach to take him and the women to the farm and to collect some supplies on the way.

Patrick saw the coach coming down the entry road and walked out to meet them. The women soon started dusting and uncovering the furniture. Michael and Patrick were given sweeping tasks. The farm house was spick-and-span by late afternoon. The women sat down to tea while the men opened up a bottle of ale. They had all earned a drink.

This house was as pretty as a picture and showed a woman's touch, whereas Patrick's house had an obvious man's influence — clean but without adornments. They women decided to do the cooking in Aunt Jane's house, the men did not argue. Patrick and Michael carried out the farm tasks while the women walked and enjoyed the views.

The area had unique flowers and scrubs and rock formations. Maeve- Ann was full of energy and with the dog she wandered further than her mother but Mary was content, her family was happy, that was the main interest in her life. Michael walked with them one day and showed them where his father had hidden the Irish rebel.

He did not tell them that Brendan Devlin, the Kyneton newspaper editor, was the rebel. He took them to the cliffs and pointed out where the two constables had fallen to their deaths.

Maeve-Ann looked at him in amazement and asked 'How many other stories do you have that you have not told us?'

Her mother laughed 'He has many, he should write a book like Uncle John.' From that moment on, the book idea stayed with Michael. He had continued writing randomly, after the Report was completed, but only occasionally and with little purpose.

Keogh was actually working. He had learnt to read plans and was assisting in marking, cutting and shaping timbers. He was enjoying himself and being paid. He felt grown up, with his own money in his pocket, not his father's. James offered him an opportunity to go sailing in a boat to be delivered to the Shannon River headland. Keogh jumped at the chance. The boat skipper was strict.

He said to Keogh 'You'd being doing as I be saying or I'll be kicking you up the arse. I don't care who you be, right!' Keogh just nodded.

Half way down the river, the skipper called Keogh to him and said 'Here m'boi, see if you can be steering the boat. Watch them sails an' keep'n 'em full. Gently y'go.' Keogh was allowed to sail the boat all the way to the headland.

The skipper said 'You can be pattin' yr back, well doon ma boi.'

James had taught Keogh the basics of ship building within the month. Keogh had been eager student and had quickly absorbed the lessons explained to him. He would be sorry to leave Uncle James and Jack, but he knew they would be returning home one day soon.

They had been in Kilrush for over a month and Michael decided it was now time to head back to Victoria via Liverpool. There they would visit John Hall's family farm at Lazonby, just over a day's coach ride from the port.

A week prior to them leaving, a new priest had arrived. The day before they left Michael went to see him and presented him fifty pounds to repair the church. The Priest asked 'To what would I be owin' the pleasure of this here gift?'

Michael just said 'In memory of the Keogh's.' He turned and walked away.

The farewell with Patrick had been difficult as they knew they may never meet again. They had enjoyed the relaxation of the Irish farm life style, it was less demanding than their farm life back home — no droughts, floods or bushfires.

They moved back to the Kilrush Hotel for their final days. They had twice been guests at James home for dinner and had thoroughly enjoyed themselves.

They each promised to write to each other. Mary said she would ensure that they did. As they departed from their final dinner together, James gave Keogh a letter attesting to his training that he had received at the shipyard. James had seen to it that Keogh spent several days in each area. Keogh treasured this document. Mary would remember Bridget for her friendliness and quiet charm. She was a typical Irish Colleen with her red hair and lilting brogue of the west Counties. Mary felt sorry for Keogh he had formed a solid friendship with Jack. She would see that he wrote to him. James and his family accompanied them to the hotel and amid some tears they all said goodbye, again promising to write to each other.

The coach headed out of Kilrush to Galway. Michael had decided that the family needed to see a few more Irish towns before they returned home. They stayed for a few days on the foreshore of Galway Bay and did several trips of the surrounding area. They then headed inland to the small villages where Gaelic was mainly spoken. The old customs were still observed and the women dressed differently. At noon when the church bells rang everyone would stop work and acknowledge the Angelus, kneel and then pray.

Some villages only had a few houses. The farms were distinctive with their dry rock walls dotted throughout the countryside. Sometimes it was difficult to find accommodation in the smaller villages, their inns were strictly for drinking. There were many reminders of Ireland's glory days. Derelict castles were everywhere. Many roofless and vacant houses were obvious. Home owners paid tax on the area of the roof. If the house was unused, the owner simply had the roof removed to avoid paying the 'roof 'tax. The weather then completed the destruction of the house, it being left empty, to slowly crumble and become a ruin, with no possibility of every being repaired, very sad indeed.

They continued to Dublin and stayed at a small hotel on the Liffy River opposite Trinity College. It was a large bustling city with a monument on every corner. The Guinness Brewery was nearby on the river and when the wind was from the west you could smell the brewing process. At night one could hear the bodrum drums, the fiddles and the whistles in the taverns and the inns. They went to Temple Bar one evening and watched the dancers doing the Kerry reels and jigs. It was noisy but you could not help but tap your feet in time with the infectious beat.

They visited the University and its famous library. It was worthy of the title as the best library in the world. It was a unique city with a character of its own.

After a week of wandering around Dublin, they had a family conference and they all agreed that they had had enough of touring and would prefer to head for home. Michael booked a passage to Liverpool the next day.

The voyage was short and uneventful. On arrival in Liverpool, they found that they would have over a week to wait for a ship to Melbourne. This suited them and would allow them ample time for a visit to John's family farm.

Michael knew that his nephew, Sean Hall was living at 'Brackenshire' and learning how to manage the property. As the coach swayed along the country roads, they were surprised to see that the farmlands and the surrounding areas were similar to the Kyneton district. Stone cottages, Hawthorn hedges, narrow roads but the paddocks were smaller and the sheep were leaner but had longer fleeces rather than the bulky fleeces of their Merino sheep. They stopped overnight once, finally arriving at Penrith. From there they hired a coach and driver, to take them to Lazonby — albeit the 'Brackenshire' farm.

Sean saw the coach coming up the driveway and was astonished to see his uncle, aunt and his cousins alight. Hugs, kisses and laughter predominated. They all quickly entered the farm house and sat down to refreshments and all started to talk at once. Sean held up his hand and asked question after question of his family. These were eagerly answered by his aunt. The others had stopped talking and listened. They could see Sean missed his family very much but also that he was accepting the challenges of running the family farm. He had an experienced supervising farm hand, two other permanent workers and a house maid to support him.

Sean showed them around the property and Michael was impressed with the layout and facilities it possessed. He was learning quickly and had now taken over the running of the farm and was enjoying being a successful farmer. His Aunt Maryanne was still overseeing the financial aspects of the farm, while Uncle William kept an eye on Sean's farming and stock management skills.

The property had been developed and improved by his deceased grandfather, over many years, particularly the farm house. The walls were made with blue stone and had had several rooms added to it over the last fifty years. The furnishings were all around one hundred years old and made of mahogany or rosewood with floors of polished wood with large carpet squares lain on top. The window drapes were heavy damask to keep the cold out and the heat in during the severe English winters. The den had two walls lined with shelves and filled with quality books. In the corner was a large impressive desk. This completed the picture of successful farmer and businessman. The visitors were most impressed.

Michael and his family stayed for three days before heading back to Liverpool for their voyage back home. As they said their goodbyes, one could see the sadness in Sean eyes. He kept waving to them as they headed down the long driveway and turned onto the road with a farm hand driving them to Penrith for their coach trip to Liverpool. They spent their last day in Liverpool sight-seeing but their thoughts were only about going home.

The SS London departed on time and headed south down the Irish Sea. The family stood on deck watching the English coast slip by. Would they ever see it again? The youngsters might but the adults had no intention of returning. Their sea voyaging days would be finished upon arrival in Melbourne.

The weather was cloudy with the choppy seas and they spent

most of the time in their cabin. The ship's planned first port of call would be the Canary Islands, for only a few hours, to pick up some passengers and mail and then to Cape Town for a twenty four hours stopover to collect supplies for the long trip across the Indian Ocean to Melbourne.

Michael saw Maeve-Ann sitting on deck and he noticed that she was reading the book on Animal Husbandry, which surprised Michael. He had noticed that she had helped Patrick and himself when they were grooming the horses and drenching the sheep. Perhaps she would become the next farmer in the family. Keogh had shown little or no interest in farming.

As planned, the stop at the Canary Islands had been quick. The ship soon sailed out into the Atlantic Ocean heading south with a following north wind. The sails were full, the sun shining and the seas had a moderate swell. It was a beautiful day.

Mary read and slept, she was only interested in returning to the comfort of their home. Neither was concerned about the farm. They knew John would be watching over their interests. They had had enough of travelling and only wanted to be back in their own beds!

They arrived at Cape Town at day break. It was an imposing city, particularly with Cable Mountain showing through the mist in the background. Michael's family went ashore on the first boat. They hired a guide and spent four hours seeing the local sights and purchased a few souvenirs. When they returned to the ship, it was a hive of activity with the loading of supplies. It appeared that the supplies were mainly fresh food stocks and barrels of water. The first night out, they were invited to join the Captain's table for dinner, after an enjoyable meal and interesting conversation, they then had an early night.

The ship was clear of land when they awoke in the morning. Keogh quickly dressed and went on deck. When Michael went to join him, he saw he was conversing with an officer and pointing at the rigging and asking questions. Perhaps he would become a Navy Officer.

The seas began to get choppy and the weather overcast. The wind was from the south west and very cold. The ship ploughed into the seas, at time sending the water high over the bows and drenching the forward deck. The passengers had all gone to the security of their cabins. There was nothing to do but read and rest. This weather continued for two days. The crew brought their meals to their cabins. The Captain did not want to lose any passengers overboard and confined had them to their cabins.

The seas eventually abated, the sun began to shine and the voyage became an enjoyable cruise. Michael and his family spent most of this time on deck. Mary was reading 'Jane Eyre'. Maeve-Anne was reading 'Animal husbandry.'

Michael had become more interested in writing his life story and was now concentrating on it. Prior to their overseas trip, he had only dabbled with the writing of his story, after he had completed his detailed 'Report on North Victorian lands' the report that covered his experiences before and during his time as a Commissioner.

Keogh, as always was on the quarter deck, standing next to the Helmsman. The Captain of the SS London soon became aware of Keogh's interest in sailing and encouraged him to become involved in nautical activities. He was a good listener and he began to write a log which detailed the daily tasks he had performed with the sailors. Michael was aware of Keogh's increasing interest in a possible naval career and also of Maeve-Anne increased interest in farming.

The crossing of the Indian Ocean had taken over two weeks. They first sighted land off their port side. This being the southernmost tip of Colony of Western Australia. Keogh was now being allowed to handle the helm in light seas under the close watch of the duty Helmsman and Officer of the watch.

Keogh had been taught to watch the shape of the sails and to monitor the binnacle which enclosed the compass. He understood the compass card and the headings and the importance of holding the ship on the course plotted by the Navigator.

They continued east with the following strong westerly winds filling the sails. The seas were choppy and made walking on the deck difficult. A person had to 'feel' for the deck with each step taken. When they reach the entrance to Port Phillip Bay, they furled several sails to slow the ship's speed. When the tide was starting to flow into the bay, the sails were unfurled and the ship tacked, powering in with the tidal flow. They were soon through into the calmer waters of the bay. The ship was then headed towards the coastal town of Sorrento and turned north to sail up to Hobson Bay.

Michael enjoyed the sight of the villages on the foreshore. The sandy beaches, the white painted cottages with the green hills and grazing sheep created a serene picture. It made Michael think of Ireland with a touch of sadness. They sailed past several other ships heading south to exit Port Phillip Bay and out into Bass Strait. As the ship approached Hobson Bay he could see the outline of Macedon Ranges in the distance.

As they sailed up the bay Keogh approached the Captain and asked him if he would be kind enough to endorse his log book. The Captain not only endorsed Keogh's entries but went to his cabin and wrote a covering letter acknowledging Keogh's performance and enthusiasm but also commending him as a suitable applicant for a naval career. The Captain shook his hand and wished him well in his future endeavours. He then excused himself to concentrate on mooring his ship.

The sails were furled for the ship to slow its speed. The anchor was released with the chain clanking noisily as it splashed into the water heading for the bay's sandy bottom. Custom officers were aboard quickly.

The SS London was the only ship arriving that afternoon and the passengers were soon cleared to board their cutter and to be rowed to the pier.

The next coach to Kyneton was not leaving until the following morning, so they stayed at a Hobson's Bay waterside inn for the evening. Next morning, Michael walked along the beach, kicking sea shells as he had done as a boy in Ireland. As a Catholic he believed in the Lord and as he walked, he gave thanks that his family had all returned safely and his good fortune at having a family such as his.

Michael and the family arrived in Kyneton just on dark. In the quiet of the evening, Dinny heard the dogs barking and in the distance, the coach horses coming up the farm lane. He guessed it was them — who else would it be at this time of the day? He quickly went to the main house and boiled water for a cup of tea. He put some precooked scones into the ever-warm oven, to heat them. He knew that they would appreciate tea and scones with jam. The table was set as it was always, ready for unexpected visitors.

That's the way it was in the country. Dinny was right, Mary and the family did enjoy the small repast. Michael and Dinny went to veranda and sat there talking mainly about the farm. Dinny's report was satisfactory as Michael had expected.

He would ride over to see John tomorrow and check the financial side of the farm and no doubt talk for hours describing their visit. The family had an early night.

They were home again with memories that would last their lifetimes.

Next morning, Michael decided to have breakfast on the

verandah. Looking towards the river he saw two aborigines down by Tabu's shed. Michael was furious, he quickly finished his meal and strode down to the shed. As he approached he saw that the two aborigines were Jimmy and a lubra.

He called 'Tabu, where are you?'

A muffled voice responded 'Me sick boss.'

Michael walked into the shed and saw Tabu lying on his side.

Tabu continued slowly. 'Boss me go soon. Jimmy he know. Come wid lubra, she Warra. She work long farm some time.'

Michael looked at Jimmy and his lubra and nodded. His anger was gone. He understood. How did he know his father was very sick?

He could see that Tabu was gravely ill and would stay where he was until he died. Michael could do little for him. Aborigines could not communicate with white man doctor, it was the aborigine way.

'Do you want me to do anything for you?' asked Michael.

'Me stay long here Boss,' said Tabu very softly.

Michael did not think he would last out the week.

He looked at Jimmy and said 'Go to the farm house and ask Missus for food and milk for three fella.'

Jimmy nodded, turned saying nothing and went up the hill to the farm house.

Michael said to Tabu 'I'll come back later today.'

Tabu just lay there, looking out at the river. As Michael walked back to the house, he pondered what about Jimmy and his lubra, after Tabu died. I'll see what Mary thinks.

Mary had put some food in a bag and milk in a bottle and said to Jimmy. 'Come back when you want more food, do you understand?'

Jimmy said 'Yes missus.'

Michael walked into the kitchen, sat down and said. 'Tabu's

very sick, I'll be surprised if he's with us next week.' He paused 'Mary, could you use help with the house work, such as cleaning and the laundry?'

'Yes, at times, but not all the time. Why do you ask?'

'Jimmy has a young lubra with him called Warra. Tabu said that she had worked on a farm, I don't know what as, but it might be worth you talking with her. When Tabu goes, I'll probably keep Jimmy on the farm to help out, but I don't want an idle lubra around. She will need to be doing something useful and I thought of you and your house keeping.'

Mary said. 'I'll think about it. If she's done domestic work before, maybe she will do. But I'll need to be comfortable with her in the house. I do need help at times, but I don't want a live-in servant.'

Six days later, Jimmy appeared at the kitchen door as Mary was preparing breakfast. He told her that Tabu had died night during the night. The only aboriginal 'Ceremony' performed at his burial was Warra's wailing. Jimmy was stoic. He dug a grave under a tree near the high bank of the river and Tabu was buried that same afternoon. River rocks were placed on the grave on top of some left over thick planks from the construction of the nearby bridge. Michael, his family, Dinny with Jimmy and Warra, who would wail every now and then, stood silently for a while in memory of Tabu's involvement in their lives. The family walked back to the farm house leaving Jimmy and Warra to their grief. Michael would talk with Jimmy tomorrow about him and Warra staying on. But he would need Mary's agreement before he would offer them a job.

CHAPTER EIGHT

Succession

O ne Evening, at the dinner table, Keogh raised the subject of his interest in a naval career. He told the family that he wanted to talk to Uncle John for advice.

Michael nodded and said 'Yes, that would be a good idea. I would imagine that with his Military rank of Major he would know some Naval Officers.'

Mary asked 'How sure are you that this is really what you want, your father and I thought that you would want to become a farmer?'

Michael interrupted. 'I think we saw enough of his interest in a Naval career during our travels to be satisfied that is the career he wants'.

Mary just nodded and did not argue. She knew that if he became a sailor, she would not see him for months at a time.

Maeve-Anne had been sitting quietly but now spoke. 'I think I'll be a farmer.'

They looked at her and nodded in agreement.

Michael said 'Well, if you are sure of your career as your brother is, you have my support.' He looked at Mary seeking her support. Mary knew that the children had decided.

She answered. 'I agree that the children should select their own careers.' She rose and kissed each of the children.

The following week, Keogh visited his Uncle John, who was always pleased to meet with Keogh. He was a tall, slim, confident young man who could converse sensibly with him. One felt that this young man would make a success of his life. John saw him riding down the lane and waved. Keogh dismounted and tied his horse to the veranda rail.

Smiling he walked to John and shook his hand, saying. 'Hello Uncle, how are you today?'

John nodded and answered. 'Fine and you, to what do I owe this pleasure? Your father was only here two days ago'

'I would like to talk to you about becoming a Navy Officer,' answered Keogh.

'Come into the house, there is no one home today. The family is in Melbourne.' John took Keogh into his office.

John started 'Well you want to be a Navy Officer. Have you thought this through? You will be away from home for long periods of time and initially you will experience periods of loneliness.'

He paused watching for a reaction from Keogh. But Keogh had made up his mind. He answered 'Yes. I have considered both of those problems and I believe I could handle those situations as they arise.'

John nodded and said. 'Yes, I can help you. I know a Navy Commander at the Victorian Military Barracks. I can arrange an interview for you. You probably already know that the Victorian Government is currently recruiting to expand its military and naval contingent. You will need to start considering what information you need to know and how to present yourself.'

Keogh asked. 'I already have a log book and letters referencing my boat building and sailing experience that I gained while I was away?'

'You already have a log book and letters of support?' queried John.

Keogh then explained what work that he had been doing in his Uncle James's boatyard in Kilrush and the experience he had acquired during his sea voyages. He then explained the log book and the two letters he had received from his mentors.

John looked at him with amazement and delight. 'I wasn't

aware of your interest in the Navy, until now. That's excellent. That evidence will stand you in good stead and should enhance your prospects of being accepted with that level of knowledge and hands-on experience. But don't be complacent. Read every article you can find regarding the origin of the Victorian Navy and complement this information with a brief history of the Royal Navy. You appear to already have a good level of general maritime knowledge. I'll contact my friend within the week and get back to you.'

John then rose from his chair to make tea. They then chatted about Keogh's trip to Ireland and return. John listened intently when he spoke of his son, Sean's farming performance. Michael had already told him of Sean, but he was pleased to hear it repeated that he had settled in and was happy on the farm. It was time to go. Keogh thanked his uncle, they shook hands. Keogh mounted his horse and waving to his uncle, headed down the lane on his way home.

True to his word, John wrote to his friend, Navy Commander Alexander Blair R.N., the next day, detailing his nephew's interest in obtaining an interview for a Cadetship in the Victorian Navy and could Alexander advise the correct procedure to apply and of what should Keogh concentrate on learning. A week later a letter arrived for John from Commander Alexander Blair R.N. The envelope contained a covering letter, an information folder and an application form.

The covering letter from Alexander was in two parts. The first part was a standard letter between casual acquaintances — good to hear from John — how was his family and health etc. It finished with an invitation to dine with him the next time John was in Melbourne.

The second part confirmed that the Victorian Navy was currently recruiting personnel and it was a good time to apply.

It further explained the best way for Keogh to prepare for an interview. His advice was similar to John's plus also to know the positions/titles together with their names, of 'Who's who' in the Victorian Navy structure. It also advised that initial interviews were held on the first Monday of each month

The folder contained several recruitment brochures extolling 'Life on the Ocean Wave.' It stated that if Keogh was successful with the first interview, he would then be invited to sit the entrance examination

The last enclosure was an application form requesting his personal details, his education level and any supporting documents he wished to attach. Finally, noting that two references were necessary from prominent community leaders, attesting to his good character.

.John rode over to 'Woodlea'farm to see Keogh and hand him the information that he had received from the Victorian Navy Office. Mary served tea and scones to Michael, John and Keogh as they sat around the kitchen table. John passed the envelope to Keogh, who eagerly extracted the contents. He read the letter first, then the recruitment brochures and finally the application form. The others sat drinking, waiting for Keogh to say something. He sat quietly and then finally said to John. 'Uncle, will you be one of my referees, please?' John nodded and said 'Yes and I've already seen William Eden and he has agreed to be your second referee.'

Michael and Mary said nothing. It had finally dawned on Michael that there was a distinct possibility that his son could be leaving home soon for long periods of time — his son had grown up. Keogh looked at his father and said. 'Father, I want to apply but I still need your written permission. Can I have it?' Michael would not stand in the way of his son's efforts to have a career in the Navy. He looked over at Mary, she had not said a word, but she knew that they must support Keogh's wish. She nodded, in agreement, to Michael.

John stayed for lunch, during which time he said that he would obtain a copy of the Victorian Navy hierarchy for Keogh to learn, but he must do his own research on the history of the Royal Navy and the birth of the Victorian Navy. He could obtain these books through the local library. Keogh filled in the application form with Michael signing his permission. He attached a statement that at the interview he would present his log book and the two letters of confirmation of his experiences, signed by an owner of a ship building company and an ocean-going Sea Captain. John posted the application form on his way back to his farm.

Keogh heeded his uncle's advice and immediately started his research. He located a book in the Kyneton Mechanics Institute library, on the Royal Navy.

He then wrote a two-page summary of its history, from its establishment by King Henry VIII through to its involvement in the Australian Colonies. The history of the Victorian Navy proved more difficult. No books were available locally.

He went to the 'Observer Newspaper' and after several days he managed to piece together various articles he had found in their back copies, and compiled a similar one page summary. He reread his log book several times to refresh his memory of the tasks that he had performed, both at the ship yard and at sea on the sailing vessels. He felt confident that he would be able to impress the interview selection board. He had previously ridden over to Sunnyside farm to collect a copy of the Victorian Military and Navy Board structure and personnel from his Uncle John.

Maeve-Anne's book on 'Animal Husbandry' had been replaced by 'Farming in the Antipodes'. She had become well known around the local country town Agricultural Shows.

At weekends, she would walk behind the Livestock and Produce Judges, listening to every word they said and observing every inspection or action they performed on an animal or farm product. While she did not neglect her school work, she was more interested in learning about farming.

She had her own pony 'Star' and three merino ewes. She would soon be entering them in the Kyneton Agriculture Show. Consequently, she looked after them using all of her knowledge and skills. She rode the pony three to four days a week, training him to trot and canter as required for the Show equestrian competitions. Dinny had prepared an area of the home paddock that was level and suitable for training her pony. The sheep spent most of their time in indoor pens in the shearing shed, to ensure that their fleeces were kept clean and free of burrs and twigs and were hand fed. All the animals were feed the best of grain and fodder and the pony was groomed regularly.

Mary was proud of her two children. They were happy, energetic and looking forward to their futures. Michael was a good man, the farm was successful and they each were enjoying good health. She had good friends, she felt content with her lot in life.

Michael visited Kyneton most days, to collect the mail and the newspapers.

Keogh's eagerly awaited letter duly arrived.

The letter was official and addressed to —

Keogh John Somerset

'Woodlea Farm'

Kyneton.

Michael called Keogh from his room and handed him the letter. As expected, the letter was from the Victorian Navy Office in Melbourne. It stated that 'An interview had been arranged for you in ten days' time at the Victoria Military Barracks at 1 pm. Please respond by return mail your acceptance or otherwise.'

Keogh wrote an answer of acceptance that evening and posted the letter the next morning.

Michael decided to take Keogh to Melbourne the night before the interview. This would ensure that Keogh would have had a good night's sleep and be relaxed. Both Mary and Maeve-Anne kissed him and wished him 'Good luck' as they left the house.

He turned and waved from the gig, Michael did the driving and they left the gig at the stables next to the Kyneton Police Barracks and then travelled to Melbourne by train. The train trip was quicker and more comfortable than the Cobb and Co coach.

Next morning, after a comfortable night's sleep, Michael took Keogh by a hansom cab to the Barracks. He wished Keogh 'Good luck' and gave him some money to get a cab back to the Hotel after the interview. At 12.50 pm, he walked up the pathway to the main entry.

Mary had ensured that Keogh was well groomed when he left the farm and that he was dressed in a suit, freshly ironed shirt and polished shoes for the interview. He walked to the doorman, all neat and tidy, and presented his letter to an official-looking doorman.

He was taken to a small waiting room where two other persons were seated. He sat down holding his supporting documents, feeling apprehensive but confident. It was nearly thirty minutes before he called.

A uniformed escort entered the room and called 'Keogh Somerset.' Keogh stood up.

'Please follow me,' said the escort.

He led him to a large impressive door, while explaining that some previous interviews had exceeded their expected duration, hence the delay. He knocked on the door.

A voice called 'Enter.'

His escort opened the door for Keogh. He stepped back and gestured Keogh to enter. When he entered the room, he saw in front of him a table with three uniformed officers seated. A vacant chair was facing the table.

An officer seated at one end rose and walked to him, shook his hand, saying 'Welcome Mr. Somerset. Please be seated.' He then returned to his seat at the table.

The man in the middle smiled and then spoke. 'Good morning and welcome again. I am Commander James. I will be conducting the interview, assisted by, on my right is Lieutenant Smith and on my left is Lieutenant Rose.'

He paused 'Did you have a good trip to Melbourne?'

'Yes. Thank you, Sir,' answered Keogh

Commander continued. 'I see on your application that one of your referees is Major John Hall.'

'Yes Sir, he is my uncle,' said Keogh.

'I met him several years ago at a Government House function. He is a fine Officer.' The Commander paused and then said 'This interview is to determine the depth of your interest and enthusiasm to join the Navy together with what knowledge you have of the Navy. Your application indicates that you have some supporting documents, may we see them now?'

As Keogh extracted them, Lieutenant Rose came forward to collect them and then hand them to the Commander. The Commander glanced at the two letters and handed them to his assistants. He then began reading the contents of the log.

He said a few quiet 'Ums'

After about one minute he looked up saying 'You certainly have acquired some maritime experience for one so young.'

Keogh said 'Yes Sir.'

He handed the log to Lieutenant Smith. After a short time he asked 'What size boats were you in involved building.'

'The biggest was a two masted fifty feet ocean-going fishing boat. Most were around thirty feet long, Sir,' replied Keogh.

Lieutenant Rose then asked 'Can you read drawings?'

The Commander interrupted, pointing to the log 'Yes. It says it here.'

'Your submission already shows your focus on a Navy career, so we will dispense with that part of the interview.' continued the Commander.

Lieutenant Rose then asked 'What do you know of the origin of the Victorian Navy?' Keogh took a deep breath and started to relate what he had learnt from the Observer newspaper. First he spoke about the arrival of the first Victorian Navy Warship on the 31st of May 1856 — the HMCS Victoria and her role in the Maori Wars. He then spoke on the Colonial Navy Defence Act and finished his answer by naming the Senior Navy personnel.

The Commander smiled and said 'Well done, we did have some other questions for you but you have already answered most them.'

Lieutenant Rose then asked several questions on local issues. Keogh handled them with ease. He normally read the weekly local and Melbourne newspapers.

The Commander then requested 'Thank you, would you leave the room now Mr Somerset? We will call you back and give you our decision.'

Keogh stood, nodded to them and left the room and returned to the same waiting room as before and sat down. Keogh felt that he had answered all their questions but he was a bit concerned that the interview was so short. Had he done something wrong? He did not have long to wait for an answer.

The same escort returned and nodded to him to follow him. The same knock on the door and the same stern voice 'Enter.'

He entered the interview room. The Commander gestured to him to be seated. This time the escort had followed him in.

'Mr. Somerset, what did you think of your interview?'

Keogh thought for a moment, he had not expected this question. He replied 'I answered your questions the way that I thought you would expect.'

The Commander nodded and said 'That's an interesting answer.' He paused

'I am pleased to advise you that you have been successful with your interview and we will be in contact with you advising where and when the examinations are to be held, probably within the month. Do you have any questions you wish to ask?'

'No thank you Sir, I have no questions.' He stood up went to the table and shook each interviewer's hand saying 'Thank you, Sir.'

He was then escorted out of the room and with a handshake from the escort Keogh left the building and hailed a passing hansom cab

During the trip back to the Hotel, he reflected on the interview. He had been confident and had expected it to be longer and more searching. But he knew that he had acquired more maritime experience than other young men of his age would have had. The interview was successful, but what of the written examination? He had been told that it would be in two parts, a written examination and a practical test.

The written part was to consist of Mathematics, English and British Military History. Keogh was fairly confident of the practical test. He felt he would perform well, due to his previous hands-on sailing experience. However the written examination was of concern, particularly Mathematics. He had passed his school mathematics examination, only just.

His father was sitting at a window of the hotel restaurant and had seen Keogh alight from the Hansom Cab. Michael stood up to greet his son, who he could see was beaming with delight.

He laughed and said 'Well done my boy, you have passed. I

can see it by your smile. They shook hands then sat down, with Michael saying 'Well tell me all about the interview.'

Keogh poured a cup of tea. He had not realised that his mouth was so dry. 'Well father, it was not difficult. They asked a few questions but they were more interested in my log book and the letters of support. I now have to sit a written examination and then carry out a practical test. They will notify me of the date. Uncle John's advice was of value, they asked me about the history of our Colony's Navy and I included the names and the positions of the senior Navy Staff. They liked my answer.'

Michael and Keogh stayed in Melbourne that night and travelled back to Kyneton the following morning, collected their gig and reached the farm late afternoon. Mary hugged her son, kissed Michael and they all went out to the veranda. Mary sat quietly next to Keogh as he related the story of the interview again.

She smiled and said. 'I knew you would succeed.'

Michael asked 'Where is Maeve-Anne?' Mary said 'She's at the Kyneton Agriculture Showground preparing for tomorrow's equestrian competition and then she's going to exhibit her sheep. There's no doubt that she will be the farmer of the family. She won't be home tonight, she's sleeping at the showground and knowing her she'll probably sleep with the sheep. Some of her friends do. She'll be safe.'

She would be pleased with Keogh's success.

Next morning the family drove to the showground to support Maeve-Anne. The arena was a typical country scene, the green grass, hay and the competitors milling around and with the various livestock completing the picture. They located Maeve-Anne in the sheep pavilion removing straw from the sheep's fleeces.

She looked up and smiled and said 'Hello family' looking at Keogh she asked 'How did the interview go?' When he told her, she kissed him on the cheek and gave him a hug saying 'I knew you could do it. Now I'll show you what I can do.' She paused. 'I hope!' After preparing the sheep she went to her pony. He had already been groomed and had his hooves painted with shiny black dye. Maeve-Anne had entered in a skilled riding competition, which was due to start within thirty minutes.

Michael's family wished her good luck and they then went to find seats in the grandstand. Promptly, on the hour the competitors rode into the arena. They rode, in single file, around the upper section of the arena in a circle. The lower section was being used to judge cattle.

The competitors were called out to individually perform several manoeuvres including cantering, trotting, reversing and turning. The family loudly clapped Maeve-Anne's efforts. They all agreed that she done very well, however she only finished third and was awarded the green sash. She was disappointed but still she was comfortable with her performance, as this was her first competition. There were the sheep competitions to come and she was confident of success.

Maeve-Anne had entered one sheep in the fine wool class and two sheep in the best pair. While her hopes had been high, she was unsuccessful in the fine wool class but she did receive another third in the best pair competition .The family agreed that she had done very well at her first Agricultural Show. During the Grand Parade she proudly rode 'Star' with her two green sashes around his neck.

Keogh waited anxiously for his letter from the Navy and when he saw his father riding up the driveway waving a letter he knew his examinations days would be soon. The letter advised him that he was to attend the Victorian Military Barracks at noon in two weeks' time and bring clothing sufficient for three days. His first examination would be at 3 pm. He had been brushing up on his Mathematics, English and British Military History and Uncle John had supplied some books he had used for his cadet examinations. Keogh had also reread his sea logs several times. He felt that he was prepared as well as he could be.

Upon arrival, at the Barracks, an orderly escorted him into a dormitory and had shown him to a bed with a locker and advised that this was where he would be staying during his time there. He was then shown where the toilets and showers were located. The orderly pointed out the location of the examination room and he had then taken him to the dining room and advised the dining times. He was led to a table and waited on by a uniformed sailor. He was early and dined by himself.

After lunch he took the opportunity to walk along the long corridor and view the wall hangings. They ranged from large paintings of both land and sea battles together with memorabilia in tall glass cabinets. Several paintings of Admirals and Captains completed the impressive display.

Keogh found a seat in a quiet section of the hall and sat quietly waiting to be called. Five other youths of his age had also congregated near the examination room. They were then introduced to each other by the orderly.

At 2.55 pm sharp the door was opened by the orderly, who said 'Please take a seat in the examination room, Gentlemen.' There were six small tables and chairs each with a folder on the desk. They were spaced at about eight feet apart.

There were two Officers seated at a table facing the examinees. 'Gentleman, you will have three hours to complete the three examinations in your folder. It goes without saying keep your answers brief but without leaving out essential detail.' said the first Officer. 'If you have a query, raise your left hand. Lt Miles will come to your desk. You may start now.'

The three hours were like a blur. When Keogh was asked by

his father, what were the questions, he could hardly remember. He had completed the three papers with 15 minutes to spare and was visibly perspiring.

Only one candidate did not finish on time, he took another 10 minutes. The orderly advised them that they were free to leave the examination room, and to be at the main entrance door tomorrow by 9 am and be ready to leave for the practical examination.

Keogh went to the dormitory, as did the others, and reclined in his bedside chair. Someone said, 'I'm glad that's over, it mentally drained me, the time limit in particular.'

Keogh nodded in agreement and said 'I wonder what the practical test will be like?' No one answered but they were all thinking the same — would it be as demanding as today's examination was?

He went for a walk around the Barracks grounds, looking at the guns and carriages. The buildings were imposing. The walls had been made with large blue stone rocks and had tiled roofs. The gardens had been laid out in a uniform manner and were well tendered. Keogh's walk coincided with the sunset ritual — the lowering of the flag. The drill performed by the Military Guard was most impressive. Keogh decided then and there that this was the career that he wanted. He would do his very best tomorrow to show his seamanship skills,

After dining, he went to the dormitory mentally tired but content and slept soundly. He and the others were unprepared for the morning bugle call which rudely awakened them at 7 am. After performing their toiletries and partaking breakfast they assembled at the main door. A large horse-drawn carriage pulled up with three sailors and an Officer already aboard. He gestured them to board the carriage, the candidates climbed up not saying a word. On the trip to the Navy wharf they could see the sea and that the wind was up and generating some sea spray. The Officer walked with them to three small single mast boats.

The Officer said, 'From your applications I see that each of you have sailed before. Which is good as you can see, you will all get wet today. Two of you candidates will sail with an Able Seaman and you will do as he says at all times, do you understand? One of you will handle the rudder and the other the sail as ordered by the Able Seaman. You will do one full circuit each.'

They all nodded.

He pointed to sea and said 'Away you go, around that pylon and back and then change over.' Two each of them followed a sailor to a sailboat.

Keogh was assigned to handle the sail and the other candidate the rudder with the Able Seaman sitting between the two of them. They pushed off and immediately Keogh caught the wind with the sail. The other candidate held the rudder straight and the boat rolled violently.

Keogh immediately slackened the sail rope, as the Able Seaman let lose a barrage of abuse at the candidate with the rudder. 'Are you an idiot, watch the sail, if he hadn't slackened the sail we would all be in the drink!' The Able Seaman reached over and grabbed the rudder and as Keogh tightened the sail they slowly gathered speed. When they got to the pylon the Able Seaman lent back and let the other candidate steer them back to shore.

They changed positions for Keogh's turn to steer and he was determined to sail from the shore correctly. He watched the sail as the other candidate pulled the line as the sail began to fill, Keogh angled the rudder to keep the sail full. He had a good run to the pylon and only had to tack once. On their way back Keogh took an angled course and although they all got drenched they arrived back at the beach first.

As soon as the last boat beached the Officer loaded the

candidates into the carriage and took them back to the Barracks so that they could towel down and put on dry clothes. He said nothing to the candidates. They were not sure what to expect.

After lunch they were again ushered into the examination room. There were now four Officers in the room one who was the Commander.

He said 'Be seated Gentlemen, I congratulate you on your commitment yesterday and today. I can imagine that they have been two challenging days. You will be advised of your results by mail. I can say this, you have all been successful, but some will be required to have extra training in some areas. Your letter will advise what will be the next stage of your career into the Victorian Navy as a Cadet Officer.' Keogh had achieved his goal.

The next six months was like a blur. His initial posting was to Victoria Barracks for basic training and induction. It varied from marching and parade drills to learning Queen's Regulations and Admiralty Instructions. Then Keogh was sent to England to spend two years training, ashore and 'Before the mast', serving on Man of War ships in the Atlantic Ocean and the North Sea.

He returned home as a Lieutenant, one of the first born Colonials to be commissioned in the Royal Victorian Navy — Lieutenant Keogh Somerset RVN. He enjoyed his title and wearing his resplendent uniform of navy blue and gold buttons and braid.

He often entertained his proud family with his stories of sailing in the Royal Navy Man of War ships around the British Isles and in the rough seas. Keogh had achieved his ambition to become a career Naval Officer and with his youth he would have the opportunity to climb the promotional ladder in the years to come.

During Keogh's time in England, Maeve-Anne had continued

her studies in Animal Husbandry and Agriculture, more specifically in the growing of grains.

Her interest in attending Agricultural Shows had not waned. Her horse 'Star' had improved as a show horse and had won several awards. Similarly, her sheep flock was still producing first class sheep and wool. As such she had become well known in the district and had attracted several suitors. She was now 21 years of age and a typical example of an attractive and personable young country woman. Maeve-Anne had not yet become attached to any particular person and many times returned home unescorted.

Michael often sat on the veranda with a bottle of beer and reminisced on his life. He would shake his head at his good fortune in the Colonies, considering he arrived as a convict. He would never forget the County Clare countryside and his relatives. He doubted if he would ever return and saw little reason to do so. He also knew that if he had not been transported as a convict from County Clare, he would not have achieved the comfortable lifestyle that he and his family now enjoyed.

He felt a sense of contentment with his family. Keogh had become a 'Person of Note' not only to the family but also to the district. Michael smiled when he thought of Maeve-Anne and her suitors, he knew that she was a good looking young woman and would one day marry and maybe leave the family farm but she knew that she could have the farm if she wanted it. Naturally Keogh had no interest in farming although he would continue to come to the farm when he was on leave.

Michael and John still visited each other for their monthly Sunday lunch and chatted of times gone-by. They had each reared two children — Michael and Mary had Keogh and Maeve-Anne with John and Maeve having John Jr. and Sean.

Each of the children had found their niche in life. Keogh

— a Victorian Naval Officer, Maeve-Anne — the Somerset family farm (Woodlea). John Jr. — the Hall family farm in Kyneton (Sunnyside) and Sean the Hall family farm in England (Brackenbank)

After the passing of Maeve, John had managed to continue to be active and involved with community affairs. He admired his sons. John Jr. who had become an astute farmer with an eye of both quality of produce and profit for the farm and Sean was prospering as a wool broker and managing the English farm and had twice returned home for short visits. The last time with his wife of four months, she also came from a farming family.

Michael and Mary were now content to sit on the veranda looking down to the Campapse River either reading or talking of times gone bye.

Maeve — Anne had become a successful sheep breeder and livestock judge, as well as running 'Woodlea'. Keogh was enjoying his life in the Navy but he would like to do more sea time. Unfortunately his excellent report from the Royal Navy had kept him office bound, most of the time, as a Training Officer at Victoria Barracks.

Michael had never forgotten Tabu and he often sat by the river bank, where he was buried. He was saddened by the fact that the immigration to the Colonies had so drastically changed the life and culture of the aboriginal race forever.

He was one of only a few settlers who knew this first hand from his involvement with Tabu, when they had worked together over the years.

Although John and Michael had come from very different backgrounds they had both become successful farmers and men of distinction in a district, what had once been a wilderness. They had been pioneers in the settlement of the district and it was now time for their children to continue the journey of progress and development of the Colony of Victoria.

THE END

Epilogue

THIRTY YEARS ON. The coach, Mary had used to drive the families home from the Royal Ball, was bought by a Cartwright in Kyneton to be used as spare parts for other wagons. During the disassembly of the coach, when the luggage box was removed, an old photograph fell out. When the photograph had blown from the coach those many years ago, it had lodged in under the box where it had remained undetected. Even so, after all those years, it was still in reasonable condition and the persons were still recognisable. The Cartwright looked at it and appreciating its possible significance, by the old style of clothing they each wore, he walked down the road and gave it to the Kyneton Museum. The staff framed the photograph and displayed it for all to see.

Not long after, two young women were enjoying the Kyneton museum collection, when one said 'Look at this photograph. See the olden day clothes, they all look very stern. I wonder who they were, maybe they were pioneers. I'll bet they could tell some stories.'

An elderly man with grey hair was sitting in the corner of the room and leaning on a walking stick with an insignia of the Kyneton Mounted Rifle Corp embedded in the shaft handle. He was listening to them. He just smiled, if they only knew, he mused to himself. He was wearing two medals high on the left side of his coat.

THE END

Notes

Australia The name 'Australia' was first used by Matthew Flinders in the early 1800's, but only received official recognition when Governor Lachlan Macquarie began using the name in official communiqués to Britain in 1817. This is one of the reasons why he is called the 'The Father of Australia.' In 1824 the British Admiralty charts included Australia and the Colonies.

Bailed up Held up at gun point to be robbed.

Billabong Lagoon or back water remaining after a previously flooded river level has dropped

Boil the billy A Colonial Australian term that continues today. To boil water in an open tin can to make a cup of tea.

Boomerang A flat curved section of wood about three feet long, capable of being thrown through the air to strike and kill a Kangaroo. If it missed its target, it would spin back to the thrower.

Bushrangers Outlaws or Highwaymen.

Bush telegraph Local gossip that travelled quickly by word of mouth.

Commissioner of Crown Lands	A person appointed by the Victorian Government to decide. agree property boundaries. He adjudicated in minor disagreements and issued inn or tavern licenses in remote areas.
Dampers	Bushman food. Plate size flat 'bread' substitute, made from flour and water
Didgeridoo	Hollow narrow wooden log several feet long used as a musical instrument. The native blows through the tube creating a rumbling rhythmic sound.
Hansom Cab	A horse drawn two wheel vehicle for hire in the city and suburbs, early equivalent to a taxi cab. The driver sat at the rear and it could carry two passenger inside.
Heads	Navy term for toilets. They were mainly situated in the bow of ships.
Lambing down	Celebrating the completion of a large shearing job
Laughing Jackass	Is a bird from the Kingfisher species, commonly called a Kookaburra. It has unique loud laughing sound. Often several birds will laugh together.
Major's Line	The track that Major Mitchell, an early Australian explorer, made during his exploration across Victoria. He travelled in a south west line from the Murray River to the sea and then a north east direction back to the Murray River. The name is still in use in some areas of Victoria.

Mechanics Institute	A community building established by local Shires in Colonial days as a library and meeting hall for social events in country districts. Many are still in use today.
Mia mia	Aboriginal hut consisting of bark sheets placed on cut tree branches inserted in the ground forming a tent like structure with an opening at one end
Nickname	A slang word or an abbreviation in lieu of one's given name. Mainly complimentary but sometimes derogatory.
Quart pot	A billy or a tin can in which tea water is boiled
Roustabout	An unskilled farm hand. In a shearing shed he would collect the wool and sweep the floor.
Sea Anchor	A square section of canvas with the four corners having ropes attached. If the ship cannot be steered straight, due to a damaged rudder or main mast' or heavy seas, the sea anchor is thrown over the stern of the ship. It sinks below the water, balloons open and then fills with water. It creates drag at the stern and keeps the ship heading into the seas.
Scones	A small 'cake' made of flour, salt and water only.
Scrimshaw	A whale's tooth engraved, with a nautical scene, by sailors in their leisure time

Squatters	Farmers, who took possession of lands without title and developed it for grazing live stock or growing grain..
Steerage class	Term for passengers accommodated in the rear of a ship
Sundowner	An itinerant bush worker who would arrive at a homestead at sunset seeking a meal and a bed.
Swag	A bushman's bed roll. In it he packs all of possessions, clothes and cooking utensils etc and carries it on his shoulder.
Tacking	Angling a ship's sail to move the vessel forward into a wind.
Tack room	Room alongside a stable, used to stow bridles, reins, harnesses, saddles and horse blankets etc.
Tartan	A Celtic colour design unique to clans. Skirts, bonnets, trousers and scarves were made to this colour scheme.
Victorian Navy	In 1865 the Colonial Naval Defence Act allowed for establishment of Colony naval forces separate from the Royal Navy to purchase ships and recruit personnel. In 1871 the HMVS Cerberus, Victoria's Warship arrived.
Walkabout	Aborigines were prone to leave their camp or work place, without warning, to go wandering throughout the countryside for weeks or months — or go 'Walkabout'.

About the Author

John P F Lynch has written several History Books and a Biography. This is his second Novel. His first Novel, 'The Convict and the Soldier' is a story of the Colony in the 1860's. This Novel is a sequel. His mother's great, great Grandparents all settled near the town of Kyneton — Victoria, during the years of 1844-1855. John was a member of both the Kyneton and Romsey Historical Societies, both of who have helped him in his research for his books.

He has travelled extensively in his career in Aviation and visited County Clare in Ireland and Cumbria in England to research his books.

John is a Member of the Order of Australia, a Knight Hospitaller of the Order of St. John of Jerusalem and a Fellow of the Royal Victorian Association of Honorary Justices. He served in the RAN Fleet Air Arm and was the President of the Romsey/Lancefield RSL for nine years. He is also a former President and Secretary of the Romsey Football/Netball Club.

Currently he is active with the Macedon Ranges Legacy Group, having served a term as Chairman of the Group, a Board Member of the Bendigo Club and is the long standing Sergeant at Arms the State Vice President of the Malayan Borneo Veterans Association and Vice President of the Craigieburn War Memorial and Remembrance Committee.

He has now retired but continues as a volunteer in the community.

OTHER BOOKS WRITTEN BY —
JOHN P. F. LYNCH

Joseph Hall — Kyneton Pioneer

A Lifetime's Journey (1935 — 2009)

Celebration of the Catholic Church
(Lancefield and Romsey 1856 -2006)

History of the Romsey Football/ Netball Club (1879 — 2009)

Romsey/LancefieldRSL Sub Branch (1933- 2008)

The Convict and the Soldier

www.ingramcontent.com/pod-product-compliance
Lightning Source LLC
Chambersburg PA
CBHW030921090426
42737CB00007B/279